SUPREME COURT OF THE UNITED STATES

Syllabus

DISTRICT OF COLUMBIA ET AL. *v.* HELLER

CERTIORARI TO THE UNITED STATES COURT OF APPEALS FOR THE DISTRICT OF COLUMBIA CIRCUIT

No. 07–290.   Argued March 18, 2008—Decided June 26, 2008

District of Columbia law bans handgun possession by making it a crime
to carry an unregistered firearm and prohibiting the registration of
handguns; provides separately that no person may carry an unlicensed handgun, but authorizes the police chief to issue 1-year licenses; and requires residents to keep lawfully owned firearms
unloaded and disassembled or bound by a trigger lock or similar device. Respondent Heller, a D. C. special policeman, applied to register a handgun he wished to keep at home, but the District refused.
He filed this suit seeking, on Second Amendment grounds, to enjoin
the city from enforcing the bar on handgun registration, the licensing
requirement insofar as it prohibits carrying an unlicensed firearm in
the home, and the trigger-lock requirement insofar as it prohibits the
use of functional firearms in the home. The District Court dismissed
the suit, but the D. C. Circuit reversed, holding that the Second
Amendment protects an individual's right to possess firearms and
that the city's total ban on handguns, as well as its requirement that
firearms in the home be kept nonfunctional even when necessary for
self-defense, violated that right.

Held:

1. The Second Amendment protects an individual right to possess a
firearm unconnected with service in a militia, and to use that arm for
traditionally lawful purposes, such as self-defense within the home.
Pp. 2–53.

(a) The Amendment's prefatory clause announces a purpose, but
does not limit or expand the scope of the second part, the operative
clause.   The operative clause's text and history demonstrate that it
connotes an individual right to keep and bear arms. Pp. 2–22.

(b) The prefatory clause comports with the Court's interpretation

Syllabus

of the operative clause. The "militia" comprised all males physically capable of acting in concert for the common defense. The Antifederalists feared that the Federal Government would disarm the people in order to disable this citizens' militia, enabling a politicized standing army or a select militia to rule. The response was to deny Congress power to abridge the ancient right of individuals to keep and bear arms, so that the ideal of a citizens' militia would be preserved. Pp. 22–28.

(c) The Court's interpretation is confirmed by analogous arms-bearing rights in state constitutions that preceded and immediately followed the Second Amendment. Pp. 28–30.

(d) The Second Amendment's drafting history, while of dubious interpretive worth, reveals three state Second Amendment proposals that unequivocally referred to an individual right to bear arms. Pp. 30–32.

(e) Interpretation of the Second Amendment by scholars, courts and legislators, from immediately after its ratification through the late 19th century also supports the Court's conclusion. Pp. 32–47.

(f) None of the Court's precedents forecloses the Court's interpretation. Neither *United States* v. *Cruikshank*, 92 U. S. 542, 553, nor *Presser* v. *Illinois*, 116 U. S. 252, 264–265, refutes the individual-rights interpretation. *United States* v. *Miller*, 307 U. S. 174, does not limit the right to keep and bear arms to militia purposes, but rather limits the type of weapon to which the right applies to those used by the militia, *i.e.*, those in common use for lawful purposes. Pp. 47–54.

2. Like most rights, the Second Amendment right is not unlimited. It is not a right to keep and carry any weapon whatsoever in any manner whatsoever and for whatever purpose: For example, concealed weapons prohibitions have been upheld under the Amendment or state analogues. The Court's opinion should not be taken to cast doubt on longstanding prohibitions on the possession of firearms by felons and the mentally ill, or laws forbidding the carrying of firearms in sensitive places such as schools and government buildings, or laws imposing conditions and qualifications on the commercial sale of arms. *Miller*'s holding that the sorts of weapons protected are those "in common use at the time" finds support in the historical tradition of prohibiting the carrying of dangerous and unusual weapons. Pp. 54–56.

3. The handgun ban and the trigger-lock requirement (as applied to self-defense) violate the Second Amendment. The District's total ban on handgun possession in the home amounts to a prohibition on an entire class of "arms" that Americans overwhelmingly choose for the lawful purpose of self-defense. Under any of the standards of scrutiny the Court has applied to enumerated constitutional rights, this

prohibition—in the place where the importance of the lawful defense of self, family, and property is most acute—would fail constitutional muster. Similarly, the requirement that any lawful firearm in the home be disassembled or bound by a trigger lock makes it impossible for citizens to use arms for the core lawful purpose of self-defense and is hence unconstitutional. Because Heller conceded at oral argument that the D. C. licensing law is permissible if it is not enforced arbitrarily and capriciously, the Court assumes that a license will satisfy his prayer for relief and does not address the licensing requirement. Assuming he is not disqualified from exercising Second Amendment rights, the District must permit Heller to register his handgun and must issue him a license to carry it in the home. Pp. 56–64.

478 F. 3d 370, affirmed.

SCALIA, J., delivered the opinion of the Court, in which ROBERTS, C. J., and KENNEDY, THOMAS, and ALITO, JJ., joined. STEVENS, J., filed a dissenting opinion, in which SOUTER, GINSBURG, and BREYER, JJ., joined. BREYER, J., filed a dissenting opinion, in which STEVENS, SOUTER, and GINSBURG, JJ., joined.

SUPREME COURT OF THE UNITED STATES

No. 07–290

DISTRICT OF COLUMBIA, ET AL., PETITIONERS *v.* DICK ANTHONY HELLER

ON WRIT OF CERTIORARI TO THE UNITED STATES COURT OF APPEALS FOR THE DISTRICT OF COLUMBIA CIRCUIT

[June 26, 2008]

JUSTICE SCALIA delivered the opinion of the Court.

We consider whether a District of Columbia prohibition on the possession of usable handguns in the home violates the Second Amendment to the Constitution.

I

The District of Columbia generally prohibits the possession of handguns. It is a crime to carry an unregistered firearm, and the registration of handguns is prohibited. See D. C. Code §§7–2501.01(12), 7–2502.01(a), 7–2502.02(a)(4) (2001). Wholly apart from that prohibition, no person may carry a handgun without a license, but the chief of police may issue licenses for 1-year periods. See §§22–4504(a), 22–4506. District of Columbia law also requires residents to keep their lawfully owned firearms, such as registered long guns, "unloaded and disassembled or bound by a trigger lock or similar device" unless they are located in a place of business or are being used for lawful recreational activities. See §7–2507.02.[1]

---

[1] There are minor exceptions to all of these prohibitions, none of which is relevant here.

Respondent Dick Heller is a D. C. special police officer authorized to carry a handgun while on duty at the Federal Judicial Center. He applied for a registration certificate for a handgun that he wished to keep at home, but the District refused. He thereafter filed a lawsuit in the Federal District Court for the District of Columbia seeking, on Second Amendment grounds, to enjoin the city from enforcing the bar on the registration of handguns, the licensing requirement insofar as it prohibits the carrying of a firearm in the home without a license, and the trigger-lock requirement insofar as it prohibits the use of "functional firearms within the home." App. 59a. The District Court dismissed respondent's complaint, see *Parker* v. *District of Columbia*, 311 F. Supp. 2d 103, 109 (2004). The Court of Appeals for the District of Columbia Circuit, construing his complaint as seeking the right to render a firearm operable and carry it about his home in that condition only when necessary for self-defense,[2] reversed, see *Parker* v. *District of Columbia*, 478 F. 3d 370, 401 (2007). It held that the Second Amendment protects an individual right to possess firearms and that the city's total ban on handguns, as well as its requirement that firearms in the home be kept nonfunctional even when necessary for self-defense, violated that right. See *id.*, at 395, 399–401. The Court of Appeals directed the District Court to enter summary judgment for respondent.

We granted certiorari. 552 U. S. ___ (2007).

II

We turn first to the meaning of the Second Amendment.

A

The Second Amendment provides: "A well regulated Militia, being necessary to the security of a free State, the right of the people to keep and bear Arms, shall not be

---

[2] That construction has not been challenged here.

infringed." In interpreting this text, we are guided by the principle that "[t]he Constitution was written to be understood by the voters; its words and phrases were used in their normal and ordinary as distinguished from technical meaning." *United States* v. *Sprague*, 282 U. S. 716, 731 (1931); see also *Gibbons* v. *Ogden*, 9 Wheat. 1, 188 (1824). Normal meaning may of course include an idiomatic meaning, but it excludes secret or technical meanings that would not have been known to ordinary citizens in the founding generation.

The two sides in this case have set out very different interpretations of the Amendment. Petitioners and today's dissenting Justices believe that it protects only the right to possess and carry a firearm in connection with militia service. See Brief for Petitioners 11–12; *post*, at 1 (STEVENS, J., dissenting). Respondent argues that it protects an individual right to possess a firearm unconnected with service in a militia, and to use that arm for traditionally lawful purposes, such as self-defense within the home. See Brief for Respondent 2–4.

The Second Amendment is naturally divided into two parts: its prefatory clause and its operative clause. The former does not limit the latter grammatically, but rather announces a purpose. The Amendment could be rephrased, "Because a well regulated Militia is necessary to the security of a free State, the right of the people to keep and bear Arms shall not be infringed." See J. Tiffany, A Treatise on Government and Constitutional Law §585, p. 394 (1867); Brief for Professors of Linguistics and English as *Amici Curiae* 3 (hereinafter Linguists' Brief). Although this structure of the Second Amendment is unique in our Constitution, other legal documents of the founding era, particularly individual-rights provisions of state constitutions, commonly included a prefatory statement of purpose. See generally Volokh, The Commonplace Second Amendment, 73 N. Y. U. L. Rev. 793, 814–821

(1998).

Logic demands that there be a link between the stated purpose and the command. The Second Amendment would be nonsensical if it read, "A well regulated Militia, being necessary to the security of a free State, the right of the people to petition for redress of grievances shall not be infringed." That requirement of logical connection may cause a prefatory clause to resolve an ambiguity in the operative clause ("The separation of church and state being an important objective, the teachings of canons shall have no place in our jurisprudence." The preface makes clear that the operative clause refers not to canons of interpretation but to clergymen.) But apart from that clarifying function, a prefatory clause does not limit or expand the scope of the operative clause. See F. Dwarris, A General Treatise on Statutes 268–269 (P. Potter ed. 1871) (hereinafter Dwarris); T. Sedgwick, The Interpretation and Construction of Statutory and Constitutional Law 42–45 (2d ed. 1874).[3] "'It is nothing unusual in acts . . . for the enacting part to go beyond the preamble; the remedy often extends beyond the particular act or mischief which first suggested the necessity of the law.'" J. Bishop,

---

[3] As Sutherland explains, the key 18th-century English case on the effect of preambles, *Copeman* v. *Gallant*, 1 P. Wms. 314, 24 Eng. Rep. 404 (1716), stated that "the preamble could not be used to restrict the effect of the words of the purview." J. Sutherland, Statutes and Statutory Construction, 47.04 (N. Singer ed. 5th ed. 1992). This rule was modified in England in an 1826 case to give more importance to the preamble, but in America "the settled principle of law is that the preamble cannot control the enacting part of the statute in cases where the enacting part is expressed in clear, unambiguous terms." *Ibid.*

Justice Stevens says that we violate the general rule that every clause in a statute must have effect. *Post,* at 8. But where the text of a clause itself indicates that it does not have operative effect, such as "whereas" clauses in federal legislation or the Constitution's preamble, a court has no license to make it do what it was not designed to do. Or to put the point differently, operative provisions should be given effect as operative provisions, and prologues as prologues.

Commentaries on Written Laws and Their Interpretation §51, p. 49 (1882) (quoting *Rex* v. *Marks*, 3 East, 157, 165 (K. B. 1802)). Therefore, while we will begin our textual analysis with the operative clause, we will return to the prefatory clause to ensure that our reading of the operative clause is consistent with the announced purpose.[4]

1. Operative Clause.

a. "Right of the People." The first salient feature of the operative clause is that it codifies a "right of the people." The unamended Constitution and the Bill of Rights use the phrase "right of the people" two other times, in the First Amendment's Assembly-and-Petition Clause and in the Fourth Amendment's Search-and-Seizure Clause. The Ninth Amendment uses very similar terminology ("The enumeration in the Constitution, of certain rights, shall not be construed to deny or disparage others retained by the people"). All three of these instances unambiguously refer to individual rights, not "collective" rights, or rights that may be exercised only through participation in some corporate body.[5]

---

[4] JUSTICE STEVENS criticizes us for discussing the prologue last. *Post*, at 8. But if a prologue can be used only to clarify an ambiguous operative provision, surely the first step must be to determine whether the operative provision is ambiguous. It might be argued, we suppose, that the prologue itself should be one of the factors that go into the determination of whether the operative provision is ambiguous—but that would cause the prologue to be used to produce ambiguity rather than just to resolve it. In any event, even if we considered the prologue *along with* the operative provision we would reach the same result we do today, since (as we explain) our interpretation of "the right of the people to keep and bear arms" furthers the purpose of an effective militia no less than (indeed, more than) the dissent's interpretation. See *infra*, at 26–27.

[5] JUSTICE STEVENS is of course correct, *post*, at 10, that the right to assemble cannot be exercised alone, but it is still an individual right, and not one conditioned upon membership in some defined "assembly," as he contends the right to bear arms is conditioned upon membership

Three provisions of the Constitution refer to "the people" in a context other than "rights"—the famous preamble ("We the people"), §2 of Article I (providing that "the people" will choose members of the House), and the Tenth Amendment (providing that those powers not given the Federal Government remain with "the States" or "the people"). Those provisions arguably refer to "the people" acting collectively—but they deal with the exercise or reservation of powers, not rights. Nowhere else in the Constitution does a "right" attributed to "the people" refer to anything other than an individual right.[6]

What is more, in all six other provisions of the Constitution that mention "the people," the term unambiguously refers to all members of the political community, not an unspecified subset. As we said in *United States* v. *Verdugo-Urquidez*, 494 U. S. 259, 265 (1990):

> "'[T]he people' seems to have been a term of art employed in select parts of the Constitution. . . . [Its uses] sugges[t] that 'the people' protected by the

---

in a defined militia. And Justice Stevens is dead wrong to think that the right to petition is "primarily collective in nature." *Ibid.* See *McDonald* v. *Smith*, 472 U. S. 479, 482–484 (1985) (describing historical origins of right to petition).

[6] If we look to other founding-era documents, we find that some state constitutions used the term "the people" to refer to the people collectively, in contrast to "citizen," which was used to invoke individual rights. See Heyman, Natural Rights and the Second Amendment, in The Second Amendment in Law and History 179, 193–195 (C. Bogus ed. 2000) (hereinafter Bogus). But that usage was not remotely uniform. See, *e.g.*, N. C. Declaration of Rights §XIV (1776), in 5 The Federal and State Constitutions, Colonial Charters, and Other Organic Laws 2787, 2788 (F. Thorpe ed. 1909) (hereinafter Thorpe) (jury trial); Md. Declaration of Rights §XVIII (1776), in 3 *id.*, at 1686, 1688 (vicinage requirement); Vt. Declaration of Rights ch. 1, §XI (1777), in 6 *id.*, at 3737, 3741 (searches and seizures); Pa. Declaration of Rights §XII (1776), in 5 *id.*, at 3081, 3083 (free speech). And, most importantly, it was clearly not the terminology used in the Federal Constitution, given the First, Fourth, and Ninth Amendments.

Fourth Amendment, and by the First and Second Amendments, and to whom rights and powers are reserved in the Ninth and Tenth Amendments, refers to a class of persons who are part of a national community or who have otherwise developed sufficient connection with this country to be considered part of that community."

This contrasts markedly with the phrase "the militia" in the prefatory clause. As we will describe below, the "militia" in colonial America consisted of a subset of "the people"—those who were male, able bodied, and within a certain age range. Reading the Second Amendment as protecting only the right to "keep and bear Arms" in an organized militia therefore fits poorly with the operative clause's description of the holder of that right as "the people."

We start therefore with a strong presumption that the Second Amendment right is exercised individually and belongs to all Americans.

b. "Keep and bear Arms." We move now from the holder of the right—"the people"—to the substance of the right: "to keep and bear Arms."

Before addressing the verbs "keep" and "bear," we interpret their object: "Arms." The 18th-century meaning is no different from the meaning today. The 1773 edition of Samuel Johnson's dictionary defined "arms" as "weapons of offence, or armour of defence." 1 Dictionary of the English Language 107 (4th ed.) (hereinafter Johnson). Timothy Cunningham's important 1771 legal dictionary defined "arms" as "any thing that a man wears for his defence, or takes into his hands, or useth in wrath to cast at or strike another." 1 A New and Complete Law Dictionary (1771); see also N. Webster, American Dictionary of the English Language (1828) (reprinted 1989) (hereinafter Webster) (similar).

The term was applied, then as now, to weapons that were not specifically designed for military use and were not employed in a military capacity. For instance, Cunningham's legal dictionary gave as an example of usage: "Servants and labourers shall use bows and arrows on *Sundays*, &c. and not bear other arms." See also, *e.g.*, An Act for the trial of Negroes, 1797 Del. Laws ch. XLIII, §6, p. 104, in 1 First Laws of the State of Delaware 102, 104 (J. Cushing ed. 1981 (pt. 1)); see generally *State* v. *Duke*, 42 Tex. 455, 458 (1874) (citing decisions of state courts construing "arms"). Although one founding-era thesaurus limited "arms" (as opposed to "weapons") to "instruments of offence *generally* made use of in war," even that source stated that all firearms constituted "arms." 1 J. Trusler, The Distinction Between Words Esteemed Synonymous in the English Language 37 (1794) (emphasis added).

Some have made the argument, bordering on the frivolous, that only those arms in existence in the 18th century are protected by the Second Amendment. We do not interpret constitutional rights that way. Just as the First Amendment protects modern forms of communications, *e.g.*, *Reno* v. *American Civil Liberties Union*, 521 U. S. 844, 849 (1997), and the Fourth Amendment applies to modern forms of search, *e.g.*, *Kyllo* v. *United States*, 533 U. S. 27, 35–36 (2001), the Second Amendment extends, prima facie, to all instruments that constitute bearable arms, even those that were not in existence at the time of the founding.

We turn to the phrases "keep arms" and "bear arms." Johnson defined "keep" as, most relevantly, "[t]o retain; not to lose," and "[t]o have in custody." Johnson 1095. Webster defined it as "[t]o hold; to retain in one's power or possession." No party has apprised us of an idiomatic meaning of "keep Arms." Thus, the most natural reading of "keep Arms" in the Second Amendment is to "have weapons."

The phrase "keep arms" was not prevalent in the written documents of the founding period that we have found, but there are a few examples, all of which favor viewing the right to "keep Arms" as an individual right unconnected with militia service. William Blackstone, for example, wrote that Catholics convicted of not attending service in the Church of England suffered certain penalties, one of which was that they were not permitted to "keep arms in their houses." 4 Commentaries on the Laws of England 55 (1769) (hereinafter Blackstone); see also 1 W. & M., c. 15, §4, in 3 Eng. Stat. at Large 422 (1689) ("[N]o Papist . . . shall or may have or keep in his House . . . any Arms . . ."); 1 Hawkins, Treatise on the Pleas of the Crown 26 (1771) (similar). Petitioners point to militia laws of the founding period that required militia members to "keep" arms in connection with militia service, and they conclude from this that the phrase "keep Arms" has a militia-related connotation. See Brief for Petitioners 16–17 (citing laws of Delaware, New Jersey, and Virginia). This is rather like saying that, since there are many statutes that authorize aggrieved employees to "file complaints" with federal agencies, the phrase "file complaints" has an employment-related connotation. "Keep arms" was simply a common way of referring to possessing arms, for militiamen *and everyone else*.[7]

---

[7] See, *e.g.*, 3 A Compleat Collection of State-Tryals 185 (1719) ("Hath not every Subject power to keep Arms, as well as Servants in his House for defence of his Person?"); T. Wood, A New Institute of the Imperial or Civil Law 282 (1730) ("Those are guilty of *publick* Force, who keep Arms in their Houses, and make use of them otherwise than upon Journeys or Hunting, or for Sale . . ."); A Collection of All the Acts of Assembly, Now in Force, in the Colony of Virginia 596 (1733) ("Free Negros, Mulattos, or Indians, and Owners of Slaves, seated at Frontier Plantations, may obtain Licence from a Justice of Peace, for keeping Arms, &c."); J. Ayliffe, A New Pandect of *Roman* Civil Law 195 (1734) ("Yet a Person might keep Arms in his House, or on his Estate, on the Account of Hunting, Navigation, Travelling, and on the Score of Selling

At the time of the founding, as now, to "bear" meant to "carry." See Johnson 161; Webster; T. Sheridan, A Complete Dictionary of the English Language (1796); 2 Oxford English Dictionary 20 (2d ed. 1989) (hereinafter Oxford). When used with "arms," however, the term has a meaning that refers to carrying for a particular purpose— confrontation. In *Muscarello* v. *United States*, 524 U. S. 125 (1998), in the course of analyzing the meaning of "carries a firearm" in a federal criminal statute, JUSTICE GINSBURG wrote that "[s]urely a most familiar meaning is, as the Constitution's Second Amendment . . . indicate[s]: 'wear, bear, or carry . . . upon the person or in the clothing or in a pocket, for the purpose . . . of being armed and ready for offensive or defensive action in a case of conflict with another person.'" *Id.*, at 143 (dissenting opinion)

---

them in the way of Trade or Commerce, or such Arms as accrued to him by way of Inheritance"); J. Trusler, A Concise View of the Common Law and Statute Law of England 270 (1781) ("if [papists] keep arms in their houses, such arms may be seized by a justice of the peace"); Some Considerations on the Game Laws 54 (1796) ("Who has been deprived by [the law] of keeping arms for his own defence? What law forbids the veriest pauper, if he can raise a sum sufficient for the purchase of it, from mounting his Gun on his Chimney Piece . . . ?"); 3 B. Wilson, The Works of the Honourable James Wilson 84 (1804) (with reference to state constitutional right: "This is one of our many renewals of the Saxon regulations. 'They were bound,' says Mr. Selden, 'to keep arms for the preservation of the kingdom, and of their own person'"); W. Duer, Outlines of the Constitutional Jurisprudence of the United States 31–32 (1833) (with reference to colonists' English rights: "The right of every individual to keep arms for his defence, suitable to his condition and degree; which was the public allowance, under due restrictions of the natural right of resistance and self-preservation"); 3 R. Burn, Justice of the Peace and the Parish Officer 88 (1815) ("It is, however, laid down by Serjeant Hawkins, . . . that if a lessee, after the end of the term, keep arms in his house to oppose the entry of the lessor, . . ."); *State* v. *Dempsey*, 31 N. C. 384, 385 (1849) (citing 1840 state law making it a misdemeanor for a member of certain racial groups "to carry about his person or keep in his house any shot gun or other arms").

(quoting Black's Law Dictionary 214 (6th ed. 1998)). We think that JUSTICE GINSBURG accurately captured the natural meaning of "bear arms." Although the phrase implies that the carrying of the weapon is for the purpose of "offensive or defensive action," it in no way connotes participation in a structured military organization.

From our review of founding-era sources, we conclude that this natural meaning was also the meaning that "bear arms" had in the 18th century. In numerous instances, "bear arms" was unambiguously used to refer to the carrying of weapons outside of an organized militia. The most prominent examples are those most relevant to the Second Amendment: Nine state constitutional provisions written in the 18th century or the first two decades of the 19th, which enshrined a right of citizens to "bear arms in defense of themselves and the state" or "bear arms in defense of himself and the state."[8] It is clear from those formulations that "bear arms" did not refer only to carry-

---

[8]See Pa. Declaration of Rights §XIII, in 5 Thorpe 3083 ("That the people have a right to bear arms for the defence of themselves and the state. . . "); Vt. Declaration of Rights §XV, in 6 *id.*, at 3741 ("That the people have a right to bear arms for the defence of themselves and the State. . ."); Ky. Const., Art. XII, cl. 23 (1792), in 3 *id.*, at 1264, 1275 ("That the right of the citizens to bear arms in defence of themselves and the State shall not be questioned"); Ohio Const., Art. VIII, §20 (1802), in 5 *id.*, at 2901, 2911 ("That the people have a right to bear arms for the defence of themselves and the State . . . "); Ind. Const., Art. I, §20 (1816), in 2 *id.*, at 1057, 1059 ("That the people have a right to bear arms for the defense of themselves and the State. . ."); Miss. Const., Art. I, §23 (1817), in 4 *id.*, at 2032, 2034 ("Every citizen has a right to bear arms, in defence of himself and the State"); Conn. Const., Art. I, §17 (1818), in 1 *id.*, at 536, 538 ("Every citizen has a right to bear arms in defence of himself and the state"); Ala. Const., Art. I, §23 (1819), in 1 *id.*, at 96, 98 ("Every citizen has a right to bear arms in defence of himself and the State"); Mo. Const., Art. XIII, §3 (1820), in 4 *id.*, at 2150, 2163 ("[T]hat their right to bear arms in defence of themselves and of the State cannot be questioned"). See generally Volokh, State Constitutional Rights to Keep and Bear Arms, 11 Tex. Rev. L. & Politics 191 (2006).

ing a weapon in an organized military unit. Justice James Wilson interpreted the Pennsylvania Constitution's arms-bearing right, for example, as a recognition of the natural right of defense "of one's person or house"—what he called the law of "self preservation." 2 Collected Works of James Wilson 1142, and n. x (K. Hall & M. Hall eds. 2007) (citing Pa. Const., Art. IX, §21 (1790)); see also T. Walker, Introduction to American Law 198 (1837) ("Thus the right of self-defence [is] guaranteed by the [Ohio] constitution"); see also *id.*, at 157 (equating Second Amendment with that provision of the Ohio Constitution). That was also the interpretation of those state constitutional provisions adopted by pre-Civil War state courts.[9] These provisions demonstrate—again, in the most analogous linguistic context—that "bear arms" was not limited to the carrying of arms in a militia.

The phrase "bear Arms" also had at the time of the founding an idiomatic meaning that was significantly different from its natural meaning: "to serve as a soldier, do military service, fight" or "to wage war." See Linguists' Brief 18; *post*, at 11 (STEVENS, J., dissenting). But it *unequivocally* bore that idiomatic meaning only when followed by the preposition "against," which was in turn followed by the target of the hostilities. See 2 Oxford 21. (That is how, for example, our Declaration of Independence ¶28, used the phrase: "He has constrained our fellow Citizens taken Captive on the high Seas to bear Arms against their Country . . . .") Every example given by petitioners' *amici* for the idiomatic meaning of "bear arms"

---

[9] See *Bliss* v. *Commonwealth*, 2 Litt. 90, 91–92 (Ky. 1822); *State* v. *Reid*, 1 Ala. 612, 616–617 (1840); *State* v. *Schoultz*, 25 Mo. 128, 155 (1857); see also *Simpson* v. *State*, 5 Yer. 356, 360 (Tenn. 1833) (interpreting similar provision with "common defence" purpose); *State* v. *Huntly*, 25 N. C. 418, 422–423 (1843) (same); cf. *Nunn* v. *State*, 1 Ga. 243, 250–251 (1846) (construing Second Amendment); *State* v. *Chandler*, 5 La. Ann. 489, 489–490 (1850) (same).

from the founding period either includes the preposition "against" or is not clearly idiomatic. See Linguists' Brief 18–23. Without the preposition, "bear arms" normally meant (as it continues to mean today) what JUSTICE GINSBURG's opinion in *Muscarello* said.

In any event, the meaning of "bear arms" that petitioners and JUSTICE STEVENS propose is *not even* the (sometimes) idiomatic meaning. Rather, they manufacture a hybrid definition, whereby "bear arms" connotes the actual carrying of arms (and therefore is not really an idiom) but only in the service of an organized militia. No dictionary has ever adopted that definition, and we have been apprised of no source that indicates that it carried that meaning at the time of the founding. But it is easy to see why petitioners and the dissent are driven to the hybrid definition. Giving "bear Arms" its idiomatic meaning would cause the protected right to consist of the right to be a soldier or to wage war—an absurdity that no commentator has ever endorsed. See L. Levy, Origins of the Bill of Rights 135 (1999). Worse still, the phrase "keep and bear Arms" would be incoherent. The word "Arms" would have two different meanings at once: "weapons" (as the object of "keep") and (as the object of "bear") one-half of an idiom. It would be rather like saying "He filled and kicked the bucket" to mean "He filled the bucket and died." Grotesque.

Petitioners justify their limitation of "bear arms" to the military context by pointing out the unremarkable fact that it was often used in that context—the same mistake they made with respect to "keep arms." It is especially unremarkable that the phrase was often used in a military context in the federal legal sources (such as records of congressional debate) that have been the focus of petitioners' inquiry. Those sources would have had little occasion to use it *except* in discussions about the standing army and the militia. And the phrases used primarily in those military discussions include not only "bear arms" but also "carry arms," "possess arms," and "have arms"—though no one thinks that those *other* phrases also had special military meanings. See Barnett, Was the Right to Keep and Bear Arms Conditioned on Service in an Organized Militia?, 83 Tex. L. Rev. 237, 261 (2004). The common references to those "fit to bear arms" in congressional discussions about the militia are matched by use of the same phrase in the few nonmilitary federal contexts where the concept would be relevant. See, *e.g.*, 30 Journals of Continental Congress 349–351 (J. Fitzpatrick ed. 1934). Other legal sources frequently used "bear arms" in nonmilitary contexts.[10] Cunningham's legal dictionary, cited above,

---

[10] See J. Brydall, Privilegia Magnatud apud Anglos 14 (1704) (Privilege XXXIII) ("In the 21st Year of King Edward the Third, a Proclamation Issued, that no Person should bear any Arms within London, and the Suburbs"); J. Bond, A Compleat Guide to Justices of the Peace 43 (1707) ("Sheriffs, and all other Officers in executing their Offices, and all other persons pursuing Hu[e] and Cry may lawfully bear arms"); 1 An Abridgment of the Public Statutes in Force and Use Relative to Scotland (1755) (entry for "Arms": "And if any person above described shall have in his custody, use, or bear arms, being thereof convicted before one justice of peace, or other judge competent, summarily, he shall for the first offense forfeit all such arms" (quoting 1 Geo. 1, c. 54, §1)); Statute Law of Scotland Abridged 132–133 (2d ed. 1769) ("Acts for disarming the highlands" but "exempting those who have particular licenses to bear arms"); E. de Vattel, The Law of Nations, or, Principles of the Law of Nature 144 (1792) ("Since custom has allowed persons of rank and gentlemen of the army to bear arms in time of peace, strict care should be taken that none but these should be allowed to wear swords"); E. Roche, Proceedings of a Court-Martial, Held at the Council-Chamber, in the City of Cork 3 (1798) (charge VI: "With having held traitorous conferences, and with having conspired, with the like intent, for the purpose of attacking and despoiling of the arms of several of the King's subjects, qualified by law to bear arms"); C. Humphreys, A Compendium of the Common Law in force in Kentucky 482 (1822) ("[I]n this country the constitution guaranties to all persons the right to bear arms; then it can only be a crime to exercise this right in such a manner, as to terrify people unnecessarily").

gave as an example of its usage a sentence unrelated to military affairs ("Servants and labourers shall use bows and arrows on *Sundays*, &c. and not bear other arms"). And if one looks beyond legal sources, "bear arms" was frequently used in nonmilitary contexts. See Cramer & Olson, What Did "Bear Arms" Mean in the Second Amendment?, 6 Georgetown J. L. & Pub. Pol'y (forthcoming Sept. 2008), online at http://papers.ssrn.com/abstract=1086176 (as visited June 24, 2008, and available in Clerk of Court's case file) (identifying numerous nonmilitary uses of "bear arms" from the founding period).

JUSTICE STEVENS points to a study by *amici* supposedly showing that the phrase "bear arms" was most frequently used in the military context. See *post*, at 12–13, n. 9; Linguists' Brief 24. Of course, as we have said, the fact that the phrase was commonly used in a particular context does not show that it is limited to that context, and, in any event, we have given many sources where the phrase was used in nonmilitary contexts. Moreover, the study's collection appears to include (who knows how many times) the idiomatic phrase "bear arms against," which is irrelevant. The *amici* also dismiss examples such as "'bear arms . . . for the purpose of killing game'" because those uses are "expressly qualified." Linguists' Brief 24. (JUSTICE STEVENS uses the same excuse for dismissing the state constitutional provisions analogous to the Second Amendment that identify private-use purposes for which the individual right can be asserted. See *post*, at 12.) That analysis is faulty. A purposive qualifying phrase that contradicts the word or phrase it modifies is unknown this side of the looking glass (except, apparently, in some courses on Linguistics). If "bear arms" means, as we think, simply the carrying of arms, a modifier can limit the purpose of the carriage ("for the purpose of self-defense" or "to make war against the King"). But if "bear arms" means, as the petitioners and the dissent think, the carrying of arms only for military purposes, one simply cannot add "for the purpose of killing game." The right "to carry arms in the militia for the purpose of killing game" is worthy of the mad hatter. Thus, these purposive qualifying phrases positively establish that "to bear arms" is not limited to military use.[11]

JUSTICE STEVENS places great weight on James Madison's inclusion of a conscientious-objector clause in his original draft of the Second Amendment: "but no person religiously scrupulous of bearing arms, shall be compelled to render military service in person." Creating the Bill of Rights 12 (H. Veit, K. Bowling, & C. Bickford eds. 1991) (hereinafter Veit). He argues that this clause establishes that the drafters of the Second Amendment intended "bear Arms" to refer only to military service. See *post*, at 26. It is always perilous to derive the meaning of an adopted provision from another provision deleted in the drafting process.[12] In any case, what JUSTICE STEVENS would conclude from the deleted provision does not follow. It was not meant to exempt from military service those who

---

[11] JUSTICE STEVENS contends, *post*, at 15, that since we assert that adding "against" to "bear arms" gives it a military meaning we must concede that adding a purposive qualifying phrase to "bear arms" can alter its meaning. But the difference is that we do not maintain that "against" *alters* the meaning of "bear arms" but merely that it *clarifies* which of various meanings (one of which is military) is intended. JUSTICE STEVENS, however, argues that "[t]he term 'bear arms' is a familiar idiom; when used unadorned by any additional words, its meaning is 'to serve as a soldier, do military service, fight.'" *Post*, at 11. He therefore must establish that adding a contradictory purposive phrase can *alter* a word's meaning.

[12] JUSTICE STEVENS finds support for his legislative history inference from the recorded views of one Antifederalist member of the House. *Post*, at 26 n. 25. "The claim that the best or most representative reading of the [language of the] amendments would conform to the understanding and concerns of [the Antifederalists] is ... highly problematic." Rakove, The Second Amendment: The Highest Stage of Originalism, Bogus 74, 81.

objected to going to war but had no scruples about personal gunfights. Quakers opposed the use of arms not just for militia service, but for any violent purpose whatsoever—so much so that Quaker frontiersmen were forbidden to use arms to defend their families, even though "[i]n such circumstances the temptation to seize a hunting rifle or knife in self-defense . . . must sometimes have been almost overwhelming." P. Brock, Pacifism in the United States 359 (1968); see M. Hirst, The Quakers in Peace and War 336–339 (1923); 3 T. Clarkson, Portraiture of Quakerism 103–104 (3d ed. 1807). The Pennsylvania Militia Act of 1757 exempted from service those *scrupling the use of arms*"—a phrase that no one contends had an idiomatic meaning. See 5 Stat. at Large of Pa. 613 (J. Mitchell & H. Flanders eds. 1898) (emphasis added). Thus, the most natural interpretation of Madison's deleted text is that those opposed to carrying weapons for potential violent confrontation would not be "compelled to render military service," in which such carrying would be required.[13]

Finally, JUSTICE STEVENS suggests that "keep and bear Arms" was some sort of term of art, presumably akin to "hue and cry" or "cease and desist." (This suggestion usefully evades the problem that there is no evidence whatsoever to support a military reading of "keep arms.") JUSTICE STEVENS believes that the unitary meaning of

---

[13]The same applies to the conscientious-objector amendments proposed by Virginia and North Carolina, which said: "That any person religiously scrupulous of bearing arms ought to be exempted upon payment of an equivalent to employ another to bear arms in his stead." See Veit 19; 4 J. Eliot, The Debates in the Several State Constitutions on the Adoption of the Federal Constitution 243, 244 (2d ed. 1836) (reprinted 1941). Certainly their second use of the phrase ("bear arms in his stead") refers, by reason of context, to compulsory bearing of arms for military duty. But their first use of the phrase ("any person religiously scrupulous of bearing arms") assuredly did not refer to people whose God allowed them to bear arms for defense of themselves but not for defense of their country.

"keep and bear Arms" is established by the Second Amendment's calling it a "right" (singular) rather than "rights" (plural). See *post*, at 16. There is nothing to this. State constitutions of the founding period routinely grouped multiple (related) guarantees under a singular "right," and the First Amendment protects the "right [singular] of the people peaceably to assemble, and to petition the Government for a redress of grievances." See, *e.g.*, Pa. Declaration of Rights §§IX, XII, XVI, in 5 Thorpe 3083–3084; Ohio Const., Arts. VIII, §§11, 19 (1802), in *id.*, at 2910–2911.[14] And even if "keep and bear Arms" were a unitary phrase, we find no evidence that it bore a military meaning. Although the phrase was not at all common (which would be unusual for a term of art), we have found instances of its use with a clearly nonmilitary connotation. In a 1780 debate in the House of Lords, for example, Lord Richmond described an order to disarm private citizens (not militia members) as "a violation of the constitutional right of Protestant subjects to keep and bear arms for their own defense." 49 The London Magazine or Gentleman's Monthly Intelligencer 467 (1780). In response, another member of Parliament referred to "the right of bearing arms for personal defence," making clear that no special military meaning for "keep and bear arms" was intended in the discussion. *Id.*, at 467–468.[15]

---

[14]Faced with this clear historical usage, JUSTICE STEVENS resorts to the bizarre argument that because the word "to" is not included before "bear" (whereas it is included before "petition" in the First Amendment), the unitary meaning of "to keep and bear" is established. *Post*, at 16, n. 13. We have never heard of the proposition that omitting repetition of the "to" causes two verbs with different meanings to become one. A promise "to support and to defend the Constitution of the United States" is not a whit different from a promise "to support and defend the Constitution of the United States."

[15] Cf. 3 Geo., 34, §3, in 7 Eng. Stat. at Large 126 (1748) ("That the Prohibition contained . . . in this Act, of having, keeping, bearing, or wearing any Arms or Warlike Weapons . . . shall not extend . . . to any

Opinion of the Court

c. Meaning of the Operative Clause. Putting all of these textual elements together, we find that they guarantee the individual right to possess and carry weapons in case of confrontation. This meaning is strongly confirmed by the historical background of the Second Amendment. We look to this because it has always been widely understood that the Second Amendment, like the First and Fourth Amendments, codified a *pre-existing* right. The very text of the Second Amendment implicitly recognizes the pre-existence of the right and declares only that it "shall not be infringed." As we said in *United States* v. *Cruikshank*, 92 U. S. 542, 553 (1876), "[t]his is not a right granted by the Constitution. Neither is it in any manner dependent upon that instrument for its existence. The Second amendment declares that it shall not be infringed . . . ."[16]

Between the Restoration and the Glorious Revolution, the Stuart Kings Charles II and James II succeeded in using select militias loyal to them to suppress political dissidents, in part by disarming their opponents. See J. Malcolm, To Keep and Bear Arms 31–53 (1994) (hereinafter Malcolm); L. Schwoerer, The Declaration of Rights, 1689, p. 76 (1981). Under the auspices of the 1671 Game Act, for example, the Catholic James II had ordered general disarmaments of regions home to his Protestant enemies. See Malcolm 103–106. These experiences caused Englishmen to be extremely wary of concentrated military forces run by the state and to be jealous of their arms. They accordingly obtained an assurance from William and Mary, in the Declaration of Right (which was codified as the English Bill of Rights), that Protestants

---

Officers or their Assistants, employed in the Execution of Justice . . .").

[16] Contrary to Justice Stevens' wholly unsupported assertion, *post*, at 1, 17, there was no pre-existing right in English law "to use weapons for certain military purposes" or to use arms in an organized militia.

would never be disarmed: "That the subjects which are Protestants may have arms for their defense suitable to their conditions and as allowed by law." 1 W. & M., c. 2, §7, in 3 Eng. Stat. at Large 441 (1689). This right has long been understood to be the predecessor to our Second Amendment. See E. Dumbauld, The Bill of Rights and What It Means Today 51 (1957); W. Rawle, A View of the Constitution of the United States of America 122 (1825) (hereinafter Rawle). It was clearly an individual right, having nothing whatever to do with service in a militia. To be sure, it was an individual right not available to the whole population, given that it was restricted to Protestants, and like all written English rights it was held only against the Crown, not Parliament. See Schwoerer, To Hold and Bear Arms: The English Perspective, in Bogus 207, 218; but see 3 J. Story, Commentaries on the Constitution of the United States §1858 (1833) (hereinafter Story) (contending that the "right to bear arms" is a "limitatio[n] upon the power of parliament" as well). But it was secured to them as individuals, according to "libertarian political principles," not as members of a fighting force. Schwoerer, Declaration of Rights, at 283; see also *id.*, at 78; G. Jellinek, The Declaration of the Rights of Man and of Citizens 49, and n. 7 (1901) (reprinted 1979).

By the time of the founding, the right to have arms had become fundamental for English subjects. See Malcolm 122–134. Blackstone, whose works, we have said, "constituted the preeminent authority on English law for the founding generation," *Alden* v. *Maine,* 527 U. S. 706, 715 (1999), cited the arms provision of the Bill of Rights as one of the fundamental rights of Englishmen. See 1 Blackstone 136, 139–140 (1765). His description of it cannot possibly be thought to tie it to militia or military service. It was, he said, "the natural right of resistance and self-preservation," *id.*, at 139, and "the right of having and using arms for self-preservation and defence," *id.*, at 140;

see also 3 *id.*, at 2–4 (1768). Other contemporary authorities concurred. See G. Sharp, Tracts, Concerning the Ancient and Only True Legal Means of National Defence, by a Free Militia 17–18, 27 (3d ed. 1782); 2 J. de Lolme, The Rise and Progress of the English Constitution 886–887 (1784) (A. Stephens ed. 1838); W. Blizard, Desultory Reflections on Police 59–60 (1785). Thus, the right secured in 1689 as a result of the Stuarts' abuses was by the time of the founding understood to be an individual right protecting against both public and private violence.

And, of course, what the Stuarts had tried to do to their political enemies, George III had tried to do to the colonists. In the tumultuous decades of the 1760's and 1770's, the Crown began to disarm the inhabitants of the most rebellious areas. That provoked polemical reactions by Americans invoking their rights as Englishmen to keep arms. A New York article of April 1769 said that "[i]t is a natural right which the people have reserved to themselves, confirmed by the Bill of Rights, to keep arms for their own defence." A Journal of the Times: Mar. 17, New York Journal, Supp. 1, Apr. 13, 1769, in Boston Under Military Rule 79 (O. Dickerson ed. 1936); see also, *e.g.*, Shippen, Boston Gazette, Jan. 30, 1769, in 1 The Writings of Samuel Adams 299 (H. Cushing ed. 1968). They understood the right to enable individuals to defend themselves. As the most important early American edition of Blackstone's Commentaries (by the law professor and former Antifederalist St. George Tucker) made clear in the notes to the description of the arms right, Americans understood the "right of self-preservation" as permitting a citizen to "repe[l] force by force" when "the intervention of society in his behalf, may be too late to prevent an injury." 1 Blackstone's Commentaries 145–146, n. 42 (1803) (hereinafter Tucker's Blackstone). See also W. Duer, Outlines of the Constitutional Jurisprudence of the United States 31–32 (1833).

There seems to us no doubt, on the basis of both text and history, that the Second Amendment conferred an individual right to keep and bear arms. Of course the right was not unlimited, just as the First Amendment's right of free speech was not, see, *e.g., United States* v. *Williams*, 553 U. S. ___ (2008). Thus, we do not read the Second Amendment to protect the right of citizens to carry arms for *any sort* of confrontation, just as we do not read the First Amendment to protect the right of citizens to speak for *any purpose*. Before turning to limitations upon the individual right, however, we must determine whether the prefatory clause of the Second Amendment comports with our interpretation of the operative clause.

2. Prefatory Clause.

The prefatory clause reads: "A well regulated Militia, being necessary to the security of a free State . . . ."

a. "Well-Regulated Militia." In *United States* v. *Miller*, 307 U. S. 174, 179 (1939), we explained that "the Militia comprised all males physically capable of acting in concert for the common defense." That definition comports with founding-era sources. See, *e.g.*, Webster ("The militia of a country are the able bodied men organized into companies, regiments and brigades . . . and required by law to attend military exercises on certain days only, but at other times left to pursue their usual occupations"); The Federalist No. 46, pp. 329, 334 (B. Wright ed. 1961) (J. Madison) ("near half a million of citizens with arms in their hands"); Letter to Destutt de Tracy (Jan. 26, 1811), in The Portable Thomas Jefferson 520, 524 (M. Peterson ed. 1975) ("[T]he militia of the State, that is to say, of every man in it able to bear arms").

Petitioners take a seemingly narrower view of the militia, stating that "[m]ilitias are the state- and congressionally-regulated military forces described in the Militia Clauses (art. I, §8, cls. 15–16)." Brief for Petitioners 12.

Although we agree with petitioners' interpretive assumption that "militia" means the same thing in Article I and the Second Amendment, we believe that petitioners identify the wrong thing, namely, the organized militia. Unlike armies and navies, which Congress is given the power to create ("to raise . . . Armies"; "to provide . . . a Navy," Art. I, §8, cls. 12–13), the militia is assumed by Article I already to be *in existence.* Congress is given the power to "provide for calling forth the militia," §8, cl. 15; and the power not to create, but to "organiz[e]" it—and not to organize "a" militia, which is what one would expect if the militia were to be a federal creation, but to organize "the" militia, connoting a body already in existence, *ibid.,* cl. 16. This is fully consistent with the ordinary definition of the militia as all able-bodied men. From that pool, Congress has plenary power to organize the units that will make up an effective fighting force. That is what Congress did in the first militia Act, which specified that "each and every free able-bodied white male citizen of the respective states, resident therein, who is or shall be of the age of eighteen years, and under the age of forty-five years (except as is herein after excepted) shall severally and respectively be enrolled in the militia." Act of May 8, 1792, 1 Stat. 271. To be sure, Congress need not conscript every able-bodied man into the militia, because nothing in Article I suggests that in exercising its power to organize, discipline, and arm the militia, Congress must focus upon the entire body. Although the militia consists of all able-bodied men, the federally organized militia may consist of a subset of them.

Finally, the adjective "well-regulated" implies nothing more than the imposition of proper discipline and training. See Johnson 1619 ("Regulate": "To adjust by rule or method"); Rawle 121–122; cf. Va. Declaration of Rights §13 (1776), in 7 Thorpe 3812, 3814 (referring to "a well-regulated militia, composed of the body of the people, trained to arms").

b. "Security of a Free State." The phrase "security of a free state" meant "security of a free polity," not security of each of the several States as the dissent below argued, see 478 F. 3d, at 405, and n. 10. Joseph Story wrote in his treatise on the Constitution that "the word 'state' is used in various senses [and in] its most enlarged sense, it means the people composing a particular nation or community." 1 Story §208; see also 3 *id.*, §1890 (in reference to the Second Amendment's prefatory clause: "The militia is the natural defence of a free country"). It is true that the term "State" elsewhere in the Constitution refers to individual States, but the phrase "security of a free state" and close variations seem to have been terms of art in 18th-century political discourse, meaning a "'free country'" or free polity. See Volokh, "Necessary to the Security of a Free State," 83 Notre Dame L. Rev. 1, 5 (2007); see, *e.g.*, 4 Blackstone 151 (1769); Brutus Essay III (Nov. 15, 1787), in The Essential Antifederalist 251, 253 (W. Allen & G. Lloyd eds., 2d ed. 2002). Moreover, the other instances of "state" in the Constitution are typically accompanied by modifiers making clear that the reference is to the several States—"each state," "several states," "any state," "that state," "particular states," "one state," "no state." And the presence of the term "foreign state" in Article I and Article III shows that the word "state" did not have a single meaning in the Constitution.

There are many reasons why the militia was thought to be "necessary to the security of a free state." See 3 Story §1890. First, of course, it is useful in repelling invasions and suppressing insurrections. Second, it renders large standing armies unnecessary—an argument that Alexander Hamilton made in favor of federal control over the militia. The Federalist No. 29, pp. 226, 227 (B. Wright ed. 1961) (A. Hamilton). Third, when the able-bodied men of a nation are trained in arms and organized, they are better able to resist tyranny.

3. Relationship between Prefatory Clause and Operative Clause

We reach the question, then: Does the preface fit with an operative clause that creates an individual right to keep and bear arms? It fits perfectly, once one knows the history that the founding generation knew and that we have described above. That history showed that the way tyrants had eliminated a militia consisting of all the able-bodied men was not by banning the militia but simply by taking away the people's arms, enabling a select militia or standing army to suppress political opponents. This is what had occurred in England that prompted codification of the right to have arms in the English Bill of Rights.

The debate with respect to the right to keep and bear arms, as with other guarantees in the Bill of Rights, was not over whether it was desirable (all agreed that it was) but over whether it needed to be codified in the Constitution. During the 1788 ratification debates, the fear that the federal government would disarm the people in order to impose rule through a standing army or select militia was pervasive in Antifederalist rhetoric. See, *e.g.*, Letters from The Federal Farmer III (Oct. 10, 1787), in 2 The Complete Anti-Federalist 234, 242 (H. Storing ed. 1981). John Smilie, for example, worried not only that Congress's "command of the militia" could be used to create a "select militia," or to have "no militia at all," but also, as a separate concern, that "[w]hen a select militia is formed; the people in general may be disarmed." 2 Documentary History of the Ratification of the Constitution 508–509 (M. Jensen ed. 1976) (hereinafter Documentary Hist.). Federalists responded that because Congress was given no power to abridge the ancient right of individuals to keep and bear arms, such a force could never oppress the people. See, *e.g.*, A Pennsylvanian III (Feb. 20, 1788), in The

Origin of the Second Amendment 275, 276 (D. Young ed., 2d ed. 2001) (hereinafter Young); White, To the Citizens of Virginia, Feb. 22, 1788, in *id.*, at 280, 281; A Citizen of America, (Oct. 10, 1787) in *id.*, at 38, 40; Remarks on the Amendments to the federal Constitution, Nov. 7, 1788, in *id.*, at 556. It was understood across the political spectrum that the right helped to secure the ideal of a citizen militia, which might be necessary to oppose an oppressive military force if the constitutional order broke down.

It is therefore entirely sensible that the Second Amendment's prefatory clause announces the purpose for which the right was codified: to prevent elimination of the militia. The prefatory clause does not suggest that preserving the militia was the only reason Americans valued the ancient right; most undoubtedly thought it even more important for self-defense and hunting. But the threat that the new Federal Government would destroy the citizens' militia by taking away their arms was the reason that right—unlike some other English rights—was codified in a written Constitution. JUSTICE BREYER's assertion that individual self-defense is merely a "subsidiary interest" of the right to keep and bear arms, see *post*, at 36, is profoundly mistaken. He bases that assertion solely upon the prologue—but that can only show that self-defense had little to do with the right's *codification;* it was the *central component* of the right itself.

Besides ignoring the historical reality that the Second Amendment was not intended to lay down a "novel principl[e]" but rather codified a right "inherited from our English ancestors," *Robertson* v. *Baldwin,* 165 U. S. 275, 281 (1897), petitioners' interpretation does not even achieve the narrower purpose that prompted codification of the right. If, as they believe, the Second Amendment right is no more than the right to keep and use weapons as a member of an organized militia, see Brief for Petititioners 8—if, that is, the *organized* militia is the sole institu-

tional beneficiary of the Second Amendment's guarantee—
it does not assure the existence of a "citizens' militia" as a
safeguard against tyranny. For Congress retains plenary
authority to organize the militia, which must include the
authority to say who will belong to the organized force.[17]
That is why the first Militia Act's requirement that only
whites enroll caused States to amend their militia laws to
exclude free blacks. See Siegel, The Federal Government's
Power to Enact Color-Conscious Laws, 92 Nw. U. L. Rev.
477, 521–525 (1998). Thus, if petitioners are correct, the
Second Amendment protects citizens' right to use a gun in
an organization from which Congress has plenary authority to exclude them. It guarantees a select militia of the
sort the Stuart kings found useful, but not the people's
militia that was the concern of the founding generation.

B

Our interpretation is confirmed by analogous arms-
bearing rights in state constitutions that preceded and
immediately followed adoption of the Second Amendment.
Four States adopted analogues to the Federal Second
Amendment in the period between independence and the

---

[17] Article I, §8, cl. 16 of the Constitution gives Congress the power

"[t]o provide for organizing, arming, and disciplining, the Militia,
and for governing such Part of them as may be employed in the
Service of the United States, reserving to the States respectively,
the Appointment of the Officers, and the Authority of training the
Militia according to the discipline prescribed by Congress."

It could not be clearer that Congress's "organizing" power, unlike its
"governing" power, can be invoked even for that part of the militia not
"employed in the Service of the United States." JUSTICE STEVENS
provides no support whatever for his contrary view, see *post*, at 19 n.
20. Both the Federalists and Anti-Federalists read the provision as it
was written, to permit the creation of a "select" militia. See The Federalist No. 29, pp. 226, 227 (B. Wright ed. 1961); Centinel, Revived, No.
XXIX, Philadelphia Independent Gazetteer, Sept. 9, 1789, in Young
711, 712.

ratification of the Bill of Rights. Two of them—Pennsylvania and Vermont—clearly adopted individual rights unconnected to militia service. Pennsylvania's Declaration of Rights of 1776 said: "That the people have a right to bear arms *for the defence of themselves,* and the state . . . ." §XIII, in 5 Thorpe 3082, 3083 (emphasis added). In 1777, Vermont adopted the identical provision, except for inconsequential differences in punctuation and capitalization. See Vt. Const., ch. 1, §15, in 6 *id.,* at 3741.

North Carolina also codified a right to bear arms in 1776: "That the people have a right to bear arms, for the defence of the State . . . ." Declaration of Rights §XVII, in *id.,* at 2787, 2788. This could plausibly be read to support only a right to bear arms in a militia—but that is a peculiar way to make the point in a constitution that elsewhere repeatedly mentions the militia explicitly. See §§14, 18, 35, in 5 *id.,* 2789, 2791, 2793. Many colonial statutes required individual arms-bearing for public-safety reasons—such as the 1770 Georgia law that "for the security and *defence of this province* from internal dangers and insurrections" required those men who qualified for militia duty individually "to carry fire arms" "to places of public worship." 19 Colonial Records of the State of Georgia 137–139 (A. Candler ed. 1911 (pt. 2)) (emphasis added). That broad public-safety understanding was the connotation given to the North Carolina right by that State's Supreme Court in 1843. See *State* v. *Huntly,* 3 Ired. 418, 422–423.

The 1780 Massachusetts Constitution presented another variation on the theme: "The people have a right to keep and to bear arms for the common defence. . . ." Pt. First, Art. XVII, in 3 Thorpe 1888, 1892. Once again, if one gives narrow meaning to the phrase "common defence" this can be thought to limit the right to the bearing of arms in a state-organized military force. But once again the State's highest court thought otherwise. Writing for the court in an 1825 libel case, Chief Justice Parker wrote:

"The liberty of the press was to be unrestrained, but he who used it was to be responsible in cases of its abuse; like the right to keep fire arms, which does not protect him who uses them for annoyance or destruction." *Commonwealth* v. *Blanding*, 20 Mass. 304, 313–314. The analogy makes no sense if firearms could not be used for any individual purpose at all. See also Kates, Handgun Prohibition and the Original Meaning of the Second Amendment, 82 Mich. L. Rev. 204, 244 (1983) (19th-century courts never read "common defence" to limit the use of weapons to militia service).

We therefore believe that the most likely reading of all four of these pre-Second Amendment state constitutional provisions is that they secured an individual right to bear arms for defensive purposes. Other States did not include rights to bear arms in their pre-1789 constitutions— although in Virginia a Second Amendment analogue was proposed (unsuccessfully) by Thomas Jefferson. (It read: "No freeman shall ever be debarred the use of arms [within his own lands or tenements]."[18] 1 The Papers of Thomas Jefferson 344 (J. Boyd ed. 1950)).

Between 1789 and 1820, nine States adopted Second Amendment analogues. Four of them—Kentucky, Ohio, Indiana, and Missouri—referred to the right of the people to "bear arms in defence of themselves and the State." See n. 8, *supra*. Another three States—Mississippi, Connecticut, and Alabama—used the even more individualistic phrasing that each citizen has the "right to bear arms in defence of himself and the State." See *ibid*. Finally, two States—Tennessee and Maine—used the "common defence" language of Massachusetts. See Tenn. Const., Art.

---

[18] JUSTICE STEVENS says that the drafters of the Virginia Declaration of Rights rejected this proposal and adopted "instead" a provision written by George Mason stressing the importance of the militia. See *post*, at 24, and n. 24. There is no evidence that the drafters regarded the Mason proposal as a substitute for the Jefferson proposal.

XI, §26 (1796), in 6 Thorpe 3414, 3424; Me. Const., Art. I, §16 (1819), in 3 *id.*, at 1646, 1648. That of the nine state constitutional protections for the right to bear arms enacted immediately after 1789 at least seven unequivocally protected an individual citizen's right to self-defense is strong evidence that that is how the founding generation conceived of the right. And with one possible exception that we discuss in Part II–D–2, 19th-century courts and commentators interpreted these state constitutional provisions to protect an individual right to use arms for self-defense. See n. 9, *supra; Simpson* v. *State,* 5 Yer. 356, 360 (Tenn. 1833).

The historical narrative that petitioners must endorse would thus treat the Federal Second Amendment as an odd outlier, protecting a right unknown in state constitutions or at English common law, based on little more than an overreading of the prefatory clause.

C

JUSTICE STEVENS relies on the drafting history of the Second Amendment—the various proposals in the state conventions and the debates in Congress. It is dubious to rely on such history to interpret a text that was widely understood to codify a pre-existing right, rather than to fashion a new one. But even assuming that this legislative history is relevant, JUSTICE STEVENS flatly misreads the historical record.

It is true, as JUSTICE STEVENS says, that there was concern that the Federal Government would abolish the institution of the state militia. See *post,* at 20. That concern found expression, however, *not* in the various Second Amendment precursors proposed in the State conventions, but in separate structural provisions that would have given the States concurrent and seemingly nonpre-emptible authority to organize, discipline, and arm the militia when the Federal Government failed to do so.

Opinion of the Court

See Veit 17, 20 (Virginia proposal); 4 J. Eliot, The Debates in the Several State Conventions on the Adoption of the Federal Constitution 244, 245 (2d ed. 1836) (reprinted 1941) (North Carolina proposal); see also 2 Documentary Hist. 624 (Pennsylvania minority's proposal). The Second Amendment precursors, by contrast, referred to the individual English right already codified in two (and probably four) State constitutions. The Federalist-dominated first Congress chose to reject virtually all major structural revisions favored by the Antifederalists, including the proposed militia amendments. Rather, it adopted primarily the popular and uncontroversial (though, in the Federalists' view, unnecessary) individual-rights amendments. The Second Amendment right, protecting only individuals' liberty to keep and carry arms, did nothing to assuage Antifederalists' concerns about federal control of the militia. See, *e.g.*, Centinel, Revived, No. XXIX, Philadelphia Independent Gazetteer, Sept. 9, 1789, in Young 711, 712.

JUSTICE STEVENS thinks it significant that the Virginia, New York, and North Carolina Second Amendment proposals were "embedded . . . within a group of principles that are distinctly military in meaning," such as statements about the danger of standing armies. *Post*, at 22. But so was the highly influential minority proposal in Pennsylvania, yet that proposal, with its reference to hunting, plainly referred to an individual right. See 2 Documentary Hist. 624. Other than that erroneous point, JUSTICE STEVENS has brought forward absolutely no evidence that those proposals conferred only a right to carry arms in a militia. By contrast, New Hampshire's proposal, the Pennsylvania minority's proposal, and Samuel Adams' proposal in Massachusetts unequivocally referred to individual rights, as did two state constitutional provisions at the time. See Veit 16, 17 (New Hampshire proposal); 6 Documentary Hist. 1452, 1453 (J. Kaminski & G. Saladino eds. 2000) (Samuel Adams' proposal). JUSTICE STEVENS' view thus relies on the proposition, unsupported by any evidence, that different people of the founding period had vastly different conceptions of the right to keep and bear arms. That simply does not comport with our longstanding view that the Bill of Rights codified venerable, widely understood liberties.

D

We now address how the Second Amendment was interpreted from immediately after its ratification through the end of the 19th century. Before proceeding, however, we take issue with JUSTICE STEVENS' equating of these sources with postenactment legislative history, a comparison that betrays a fundamental misunderstanding of a court's interpretive task. See *post*, at 27, n. 28. "Legislative history," of course, refers to the pre-enactment statements of those who drafted or voted for a law; it is considered persuasive by some, not because they reflect the general understanding of the disputed terms, but because the legislators who heard or read those statements presumably voted with that understanding. *Ibid.* "Postenactment legislative history," *ibid.*, a deprecatory contradiction in terms, refers to statements of those who drafted or voted for the law that are made after its enactment and hence could have had no effect on the congressional vote. It most certainly does not refer to the examination of a variety of legal and other sources to determine *the public understanding* of a legal text in the period after its enactment or ratification. That sort of inquiry is a critical tool of constitutional interpretation. As we will show, virtually all interpreters of the Second Amendment in the century after its enactment interpreted the amendment as we do.

1. Post-ratification Commentary

Three important founding-era legal scholars interpreted

Opinion of the Court

the Second Amendment in published writings. All three understood it to protect an individual right unconnected with militia service.

St. George Tucker's version of Blackstone's Commentaries, as we explained above, conceived of the Blackstonian arms right as necessary for self-defense. He equated that right, absent the religious and class-based restrictions, with the Second Amendment. See 2 Tucker's Blackstone 143. In Note D, entitled, "View of the Constitution of the United States," Tucker elaborated on the Second Amendment: "This may be considered as the true palladium of liberty . . . . The right to self-defence is the first law of nature: in most governments it has been the study of rulers to confine the right within the narrowest limits possible. Wherever standing armies are kept up, and the right of the people to keep and bear arms is, under any colour or pretext whatsoever, prohibited, liberty, if not already annihilated, is on the brink of destruction." 1 *id.,* at App. 300 (ellipsis in original). He believed that the English game laws had abridged the right by prohibiting "keeping a gun or other engine for the destruction of game." *Ibid*; see also 2 *id.,* at 143, and nn. 40 and 41. He later grouped the right with some of the individual rights included in the First Amendment and said that if "a law be passed by congress, prohibiting" any of those rights, it would "be the province of the judiciary to pronounce whether any such act were constitutional, or not; and if not, to acquit the accused . . . ." 1 *id.,* at App. 357. It is unlikely that Tucker was referring to a person's being "accused" of violating a law making it a crime to bear arms in a state militia.[19]

---

[19] JUSTICE STEVENS quotes some of Tucker's unpublished notes, which he claims show that Tucker had ambiguous views about the Second Amendment. See *post,* at 31, and n. 32. But it is clear from the notes that Tucker located the power of States to arm their militias in the *Tenth* Amendment, and that he cited the Second Amendment for the

In 1825, William Rawle, a prominent lawyer who had been a member of the Pennsylvania Assembly that ratified the Bill of Rights, published an influential treatise, which analyzed the Second Amendment as follows:

> "The first [principle] is a declaration that a well regulated militia is necessary to the security of a free state; a proposition from which few will dissent. . . .

> "The corollary, from the first position is, that the right of the people to keep and bear arms shall not be infringed.

> "The prohibition is general. No clause in the constitution could by any rule of construction be conceived to give to congress a power to disarm the people. Such a flagitious attempt could only be made under some general pretence by a state legislature. But if in any blind pursuit of inordinate power, either should attempt it, this amendment may be appealed to as a restraint on both." Rawle 121–122.[20]

Like Tucker, Rawle regarded the English game laws as violating the right codified in the Second Amendment. See *id.*, 122–123. Rawle clearly differentiated between the people's right to bear arms and their service in a militia: "In a people permitted and accustomed to bear arms, we have the rudiments of a militia, which properly consists of armed citizens, divided into military bands, and instructed

------

proposition that such armament could not run afoul of any power of the federal government (since the amendment prohibits Congress from ordering disarmament). Nothing in the passage implies that the Second Amendment pertains only to the carrying of arms in the organized militia.

[20] Rawle, writing before our decision in *Barron ex rel. Tiernan* v. *Mayor of Baltimore*, 7 Pet. 243 (1833), believed that the Second Amendment could be applied against the States. Such a belief would of course be nonsensical on petitioners' view that it protected only a right to possess and carry arms when conscripted by the State itself into militia service.

at least in part, in the use of arms for the purposes of war." *Id.,* at 140. Rawle further said that the Second Amendment right ought not "be abused to the disturbance of the public peace," such as by assembling with other armed individuals "for an unlawful purpose"—statements that make no sense if the right does not extend to *any* individual purpose.

Joseph Story published his famous Commentaries on the Constitution of the United States in 1833. JUSTICE STEVENS suggests that "[t]here is not so much as a whisper" in Story's explanation of the Second Amendment that favors the individual-rights view. *Post,* at 34. That is wrong. Story explained that the English Bill of Rights had also included a "right to bear arms," a right that, as we have discussed, had nothing to do with militia service. 3 Story §1858. He then equated the English right with the Second Amendment:

> "§1891. A similar provision [to the Second Amendment] in favour of protestants (for to them it is confined) is to be found in the bill of rights of 1688, it being declared, 'that the subjects, which are protestants, may have arms for their defence suitable to their condition, and as allowed by law.' But under various pretences the effect of this provision has been greatly narrowed; and it is at present in England more nominal than real, as a defensive privilege." (Footnotes omitted.)

This comparison to the Declaration of Right would not make sense if the Second Amendment right was the right to use a gun in a militia, which was plainly not what the English right protected. As the Tennessee Supreme Court recognized 38 years after Story wrote his Commentaries, "[t]he passage from Story, shows clearly that this right was intended . . . and was guaranteed to, and to be exercised and enjoyed by the citizen as such, and not by him as a soldier, or in defense solely of his political rights." *Andrews* v. *State*, 50 Tenn. 165, 183 (1871). Story's Commentaries also cite as support Tucker and Rawle, both of whom clearly viewed the right as unconnected to militia service. See 3 Story §1890, n. 2; §1891, n. 3. In addition, in a shorter 1840 work Story wrote: "One of the ordinary modes, by which tyrants accomplish their purposes without resistance, is, by disarming the people, and making it an offence to keep arms, and by substituting a regular army in the stead of a resort to the militia." A Familiar Exposition of the Constitution of the United States §450 (reprinted in 1986).

Antislavery advocates routinely invoked the right to bear arms for self-defense. Joel Tiffany, for example, citing Blackstone's description of the right, wrote that "the right to keep and bear arms, also implies the right to use them if necessary in self defence; without this right to use the guaranty would have hardly been worth the paper it consumed." A Treatise on the Unconstitutionality of American Slavery 117–118 (1849); see also L. Spooner, The Unconstitutionality of Slavery 116 (1845) (right enables "personal defence"). In his famous Senate speech about the 1856 "Bleeding Kansas" conflict, Charles Sumner proclaimed:

> "The rifle has ever been the companion of the pioneer and, under God, his tutelary protector against the red man and the beast of the forest. Never was this efficient weapon more needed in just self-defence, than now in Kansas, and at least one article in our National Constitution must be blotted out, before the complete right to it can in any way be impeached. And yet such is the madness of the hour, that, in defiance of the solemn guarantee, embodied in the Amendments to the Constitution, that 'the right of the people to keep and bear arms shall not be infringed,'

the people of Kansas have been arraigned for keeping and bearing them, and the Senator from South Carolina has had the face to say openly, on this floor, that they should be disarmed—of course, that the fanatics of Slavery, his allies and constituents, may meet no impediment." The Crime Against Kansas, May 19–20, 1856, in American Speeches: Political Oratory from the Revolution to the Civil War 553, 606–607 (2006).

We have found only one early 19th-century commentator who clearly conditioned the right to keep and bear arms upon service in the militia—and he recognized that the prevailing view was to the contrary. "The provision of the constitution, declaring the right of the people to keep and bear arms, &c. was probably intended to apply to the right of the people to bear arms for such [militia-related] purposes only, and not to prevent congress or the legislatures of the different states from enacting laws to prevent the citizens from always going armed. A different construction however has been given to it." B. Oliver, The Rights of an American Citizen 177 (1832).

2. Pre-Civil War Case Law

The 19th-century cases that interpreted the Second Amendment universally support an individual right unconnected to militia service. In *Houston* v. *Moore,* 5 Wheat. 1, 24 (1820), this Court held that States have concurrent power over the militia, at least where not preempted by Congress. Agreeing in dissent that States could "organize, discipline, and arm" the militia in the absence of conflicting federal regulation, Justice Story said that the Second Amendment "may not, perhaps, be thought to have any important bearing on this point. If it have, it confirms and illustrates, rather than impugns the reasoning already suggested." *Id.,* at 51–53. Of course, if the Amendment simply "protect[ed] the right of the people of each of the several States to maintain a well-regulated militia," *post*, at 1 (STEVENS, J., dissenting), it would have enormous and obvious bearing on the point. But the Court and Story derived the States' power over the militia from the nonexclusive nature of federal power, not from the Second Amendment, whose preamble merely "confirms and illustrates" the importance of the militia. Even clearer was Justice Baldwin. In the famous fugitive-slave case of *Johnson* v. *Tompkins*, 13 F. Cas. 840, 850, 852 (CC Pa. 1833), Baldwin, sitting as a circuit judge, cited both the Second Amendment and the Pennsylvania analogue for his conclusion that a citizen has "a right to carry arms in defence of his property or person, and to use them, if either were assailed with such force, numbers or violence as made it necessary for the protection or safety of either."

Many early 19th-century state cases indicated that the Second Amendment right to bear arms was an individual right unconnected to militia service, though subject to certain restrictions. A Virginia case in 1824 holding that the Constitution did not extend to free blacks explained that "numerous restrictions imposed on [blacks] in our Statute Book, many of which are inconsistent with the letter and spirit of the Constitution, both of this State and of the United States as respects the free whites, demonstrate, that, here, those instruments have not been considered to extend equally to both classes of our population. We will only instance the restriction upon the migration of free blacks into this State, and upon their right to bear arms." *Aldridge* v. *Commonwealth*, 2 Va. Cas. 447, 449 (Gen. Ct.). The claim was obviously not that blacks were prevented from carrying guns in the militia.[21] See also

---

[21] JUSTICE STEVENS suggests that this is not obvious because free blacks in Virginia had been required to muster without arms. See *post*, at 28, n. 29 (citing Siegel, The Federal Government's Power to Enact Color-Conscious Laws, 92 Nw. U. L. Rev. 477, 497 (1998)). But that could not have been the type of law referred to in *Aldridge*, because that practice had stopped 30 years earlier when blacks were excluded

Waters v. *State*, 1 Gill 302, 309 (Md. 1843) (because free blacks were treated as a "dangerous population," "laws have been passed to prevent their migration into this State; to make it unlawful for them to bear arms; to guard even their religious assemblages with peculiar watchfulness"). An 1829 decision by the Supreme Court of Michigan said: "The constitution of the United States also grants to the citizen the right to keep and bear arms. But the grant of this privilege cannot be construed into the right in him who keeps a gun to destroy his neighbor. No rights are intended to be granted by the constitution for an unlawful or unjustifiable purpose." *United States* v. *Sheldon*, in 5 Transactions of the Supreme Court of the Territory of Michigan 337, 346 (W. Blume ed. 1940) (hereinafter Blume). It is not possible to read this as discussing anything other than an individual right unconnected to militia service. If it did have to do with militia service, the limitation upon it would not be any "unlawful or unjustifiable purpose," but any nonmilitary purpose whatsoever.

In *Nunn* v. *State*, 1 Ga. 243, 251 (1846), the Georgia Supreme Court construed the Second Amendment as protecting the "*natural* right of self-defence" and therefore struck down a ban on carrying pistols openly. Its opinion perfectly captured the way in which the operative clause of the Second Amendment furthers the purpose announced

---

entirely from the militia by the First Militia Act. See Siegel, *supra*, at 498, n. 120. JUSTICE STEVENS further suggests that laws barring blacks from militia service could have been said to violate the "right to bear arms." But under JUSTICE STEVENS' reading of the Second Amendment (we think), the protected right is the right to carry arms to the extent one is enrolled in the militia, not the right *to be in the militia.* Perhaps JUSTICE STEVENS really does adopt the full-blown idiomatic meaning of "bear arms," in which case every man and woman in this country has a right "to be a soldier" or even "to wage war." In any case, it is clear to us that *Aldridge*'s allusion to the existing Virginia "restriction" upon the right of free blacks "to bear arms" could only have referred to "laws prohibiting blacks from keeping weapons," Siegel, *supra,* at 497–498.

in the prefatory clause, in continuity with the English right:

> "The right of the whole people, old and young, men, women and boys, and not militia only, to keep and bear *arms* of every description, and not *such* merely as are used by the *militia,* shall not be *infringed,* curtailed, or broken in upon, in the smallest degree; and all this for the important end to be attained: the rearing up and qualifying a well-regulated militia, so vitally necessary to the security of a free State. Our opinion is, that any law, State or Federal, is repugnant to the Constitution, and void, which contravenes this *right,* originally belonging to our forefathers, trampled under foot by Charles I. and his two wicked sons and successors, re-established by the revolution of 1688, conveyed to this land of liberty by the colonists, and finally incorporated conspicuously in our own Magna Charta!"

Likewise, in *State* v. *Chandler*, 5 La. Ann. 489, 490 (1850), the Louisiana Supreme Court held that citizens had a right to carry arms openly: "This is the right guaranteed by the Constitution of the United States, and which is calculated to incite men to a manly and noble defence of themselves, if necessary, and of their country, without any tendency to secret advantages and unmanly assassinations."

Those who believe that the Second Amendment preserves only a militia-centered right place great reliance on the Tennessee Supreme Court's 1840 decision in *Aymette* v. *State*, 21 Tenn. 154. The case does not stand for that broad proposition; in fact, the case does not mention the word "militia" at all, except in its quoting of the Second Amendment. *Aymette* held that the state constitutional guarantee of the right to "bear" arms did not prohibit the banning of concealed weapons. The opinion first recognized that both the state right and the federal right were descendents of the 1689 English right, but (erroneously, and contrary to virtually all other authorities) read that right to refer only to "protect[ion of] the public liberty" and "keep[ing] in awe those in power," *id.*, at 158. The court then adopted a sort of middle position, whereby citizens were permitted to carry arms openly, unconnected with any service in a formal militia, but were given the right to use them only for the military purpose of banding together to oppose tyranny. This odd reading of the right is, to be sure, not the one we adopt—but it is not petitioners' reading either. More importantly, seven years earlier the Tennessee Supreme Court had treated the state constitutional provision as conferring a right "of all the free citizens of the State to keep and bear arms for their defence," *Simpson,* 5 Yer., at 360; and 21 years later the court held that the "keep" portion of the state constitutional right included the right to personal self-defense: "[T]he right to keep arms involves, necessarily, the right to use such arms for all the ordinary purposes, and in all the ordinary modes usual in the country, and to which arms are adapted, limited by the duties of a good citizen in times of peace." *Andrews,* 50 Tenn., at 178; see also *ibid.* (equating state provision with Second Amendment).

3. Post-Civil War Legislation.

In the aftermath of the Civil War, there was an outpouring of discussion of the Second Amendment in Congress and in public discourse, as people debated whether and how to secure constitutional rights for newly free slaves. See generally S. Halbrook, Freedmen, the Fourteenth Amendment, and the Right to Bear Arms, 1866–1876 (1998) (hereinafter Halbrook); Brief for Institute for Justice as *Amicus Curiae.* Since those discussions took place 75 years after the ratification of the Second Amendment, they do not provide as much insight into its original meaning as earlier sources. Yet those born and educated in the early 19th century faced a widespread effort to limit arms ownership by a large number of citizens; their understanding of the origins and continuing significance of the Amendment is instructive.

Blacks were routinely disarmed by Southern States after the Civil War. Those who opposed these injustices frequently stated that they infringed blacks' constitutional right to keep and bear arms. Needless to say, the claim was not that blacks were being prohibited from carrying arms in an organized state militia. A Report of the Commission of the Freedmen's Bureau in 1866 stated plainly: "[T]he civil law [of Kentucky] prohibits the colored man from bearing arms. . . . Their arms are taken from them by the civil authorities. . . . Thus, the right of the people to keep and bear arms as provided in the Constitution is *infringed*." H. R. Exec. Doc. No. 70, 39th Cong., 1st Sess., 233, 236. A joint congressional Report decried:

> "in some parts of [South Carolina], armed parties are, without proper authority, engaged in seizing all fire-arms found in the hands of the freemen. Such conduct is in clear and direct violation of their personal rights as guaranteed by the Constitution of the United States, which declares that 'the right of the people to keep and bear arms shall not be infringed.' The freedmen of South Carolina have shown by their peaceful and orderly conduct that they can safely be trusted with fire-arms, and they need them to kill game for subsistence, and to protect their crops from destruction by birds and animals." Joint Comm. on Reconstruction, H. R. Rep. No. 30, 39th Cong., 1st Sess., pt. 2, p. 229 (1866) (Proposed Circular of Brigadier General R. Saxton).

The view expressed in these statements was widely reported and was apparently widely held. For example, an editorial in The Loyal Georgian (Augusta) on February 3, 1866, assured blacks that "[a]ll men, without distinction of color, have the right to keep and bear arms to defend their homes, families or themselves." Halbrook 19.

Congress enacted the Freedmen's Bureau Act on July 16, 1866. Section 14 stated:

> "[T]he right . . . to have full and equal benefit of all laws and proceedings concerning personal liberty, personal security, and the acquisition, enjoyment, and disposition of estate, real and personal, including the constitutional right to bear arms, shall be secured to and enjoyed by all the citizens . . . without respect to race or color, or previous condition of slavery. . . . " 14 Stat. 176–177.

The understanding that the Second Amendment gave freed blacks the right to keep and bear arms was reflected in congressional discussion of the bill, with even an opponent of it saying that the founding generation "were for every man bearing his arms about him and keeping them in his house, his castle, for his own defense." Cong. Globe, 39th Cong., 1st Sess., 362, 371 (1866) (Sen. Davis).

Similar discussion attended the passage of the Civil Rights Act of 1871 and the Fourteenth Amendment. For example, Representative Butler said of the Act: "Section eight is intended to enforce the well-known constitutional provision guaranteeing the right of the citizen to 'keep and bear arms,' and provides that whoever shall take away, by force or violence, or by threats and intimidation, the arms and weapons which any person may have for his defense, shall be deemed guilty of larceny of the same." H. R. Rep. No. 37, 41st Cong., 3d Sess., pp. 7–8 (1871). With respect to the proposed Amendment, Senator Pomeroy described as one of the three "indispensable" "safeguards of liberty . . . under the Constitution" a man's "right to bear arms for the defense of himself and family and his homestead."

Cong. Globe, 39th Cong., 1st Sess., 1182 (1866). Representative Nye thought the Fourteenth Amendment unnecessary because "[a]s citizens of the United States [blacks] have equal right to protection, and to keep and bear arms for self-defense." *Id.*, at 1073 (1866).

It was plainly the understanding in the post-Civil War Congress that the Second Amendment protected an individual right to use arms for self-defense.

4. Post-Civil War Commentators.

Every late-19th-century legal scholar that we have read interpreted the Second Amendment to secure an individual right unconnected with militia service. The most famous was the judge and professor Thomas Cooley, who wrote a massively popular 1868 Treatise on Constitutional Limitations. Concerning the Second Amendment it said:

> "Among the other defences to personal liberty should be mentioned the right of the people to keep and bear arms. . . . The alternative to a standing army is 'a well-regulated militia,' but this cannot exist unless the people are trained to bearing arms. How far it is in the power of the legislature to regulate this right, we shall not undertake to say, as happily there has been very little occasion to discuss that subject by the courts." *Id.*, at 350.

That Cooley understood the right not as connected to militia service, but as securing the militia by ensuring a populace familiar with arms, is made even clearer in his 1880 work, General Principles of Constitutional Law. The Second Amendment, he said, "was adopted with some modification and enlargement from the English Bill of Rights of 1688, where it stood as a protest against arbitrary action of the overturned dynasty in disarming the people." *Id.*, at 270. In a section entitled "The Right in General," he continued:

"It might be supposed from the phraseology of this
provision that the right to keep and bear arms was
only guaranteed to the militia; but this would be an
interpretation not warranted by the intent. The militia, as has been elsewhere explained, consists of those
persons who, under the law, are liable to the perform-
ance of military duty, and are officered and enrolled
for service when called upon. But the law may make
provision for the enrolment of all who are fit to perform military duty, or of a small number only, or it
may wholly omit to make any provision at all; and if
the right were limited to those enrolled, the purpose of
this guaranty might be defeated altogether by the action or neglect to act of the government it was meant
to hold in check. The meaning of the provision undoubtedly is, that the people, from whom the militia
must be taken, shall have the right to keep and bear
arms; and they need no permission or regulation of
law for the purpose. But this enables government to
have a well-regulated militia; for to bear arms implies
something more than the mere keeping; it implies the
learning to handle and use them in a way that makes
those who keep them ready for their efficient use; in
other words, it implies the right to meet for voluntary
discipline in arms, observing in doing so the laws of
public order." *Id.*, at 271.

All other post-Civil War 19th-century sources we have
found concurred with Cooley. One example from each
decade will convey the general flavor:

"[The purpose of the Second Amendment is] to secure
a well-armed militia. . . . But a militia would be useless unless the citizens were enabled to exercise themselves in the use of warlike weapons. To preserve this
privilege, and to secure to the people the ability to oppose themselves in military force against the usurpa-

tions of government, as well as against enemies from without, that government is forbidden by any law or proceeding to invade or destroy the right to keep and bear arms. . . . The clause is analogous to the one securing the freedom of speech and of the press. Freedom, not license, is secured; the fair use, not the libellous abuse, is protected." J. Pomeroy, An Introduction to the Constitutional Law of the United States 152–153 (1868) (hereinafter Pomeroy).

"As the Constitution of the United States, and the constitutions of several of the states, in terms more or less comprehensive, declare the right of the people to keep and bear arms, it has been a subject of grave discussion, in some of the state courts, whether a statute prohibiting persons, when not on a journey, or as travellers, from *wearing or carrying concealed weapons*, be constitutional. There has been a great difference of opinion on the question." 2 J. Kent, Commentaries on American Law *340, n. 2 (O. Holmes ed., 12th ed. 1873) (hereinafter Kent).

"Some general knowledge of firearms is important to the public welfare; because it would be impossible, in case of war, to organize promptly an efficient force of volunteers unless the people had some familiarity with weapons of war. The Constitution secures the right of the people to keep and bear arms. No doubt, a citizen who keeps a gun or pistol under judicious precautions, practices in safe places the use of it, and in due time teaches his sons to do the same, exercises his individual right. No doubt, a person whose residence or duties involve peculiar peril may keep a pistol for prudent self-defence." B. Abbott, Judge and Jury: A Popular Explanation of the Leading Topics in the Law of the Land 333 (1880) (hereinafter Abbott).

"The right to bear arms has always been the distinctive privilege of freemen. Aside from any necessity of self-protection to the person, it represents among all nations power coupled with the exercise of a certain jurisdiction. . . . [I]t was not necessary that the right to bear arms should be granted in the Constitution, for it had always existed." J. Ordronaux, Constitutional Legislation in the United States 241–242 (1891).

E

We now ask whether any of our precedents forecloses the conclusions we have reached about the meaning of the Second Amendment.

United States v. *Cruikshank*, 92 U. S. 542, in the course of vacating the convictions of members of a white mob for depriving blacks of their right to keep and bear arms, held that the Second Amendment does not by its own force apply to anyone other than the Federal Government. The opinion explained that the right "is not a right granted by the Constitution [or] in any manner dependent upon that instrument for its existence. The second amendment . . . means no more than that it shall not be infringed by Congress." 92 U. S., at 553. States, we said, were free to restrict or protect the right under their police powers. The limited discussion of the Second Amendment in *Cruikshank* supports, if anything, the individual-rights interpretation. There was no claim in *Cruikshank* that the victims had been deprived of their right to carry arms in a militia; indeed, the Governor had disbanded the local militia unit the year before the mob's attack, see C. Lane, The Day Freedom Died 62 (2008). We described the right protected by the Second Amendment as "'bearing arms for a lawful purpose'"[22] and said that "the people [must] look

---

[22] JUSTICE STEVENS' accusation that this is "not accurate," *post*, at 39,

for their protection against any violation by their fellow-citizens of the rights it recognizes" to the States' police power. 92 U. S., at 553. That discussion makes little sense if it is only a right to bear arms in a state militia.[23]

Presser v. *Illinois*, 116 U. S. 252 (1886), held that the right to keep and bear arms was not violated by a law that forbade "bodies of men to associate together as military organizations, or to drill or parade with arms in cities and towns unless authorized by law." *Id.*, at 264–265. This does not refute the individual-rights interpretation of the Amendment; no one supporting that interpretation has contended that States may not ban such groups. JUSTICE STEVENS presses *Presser* into service to support his view that the right to bear arms is limited to service in the militia by joining *Presser*'s brief discussion of the Second Amendment with a later portion of the opinion making the seemingly relevant (to the Second Amendment) point that the plaintiff was not a member of the state militia. Unfortunately for JUSTICE STEVENS' argument, that later portion deals with the *Fourteenth Amendment;* it was the *Fourteenth Amendment* to which the plaintiff's nonmembership in the militia was relevant. Thus, JUSTICE STEVENS' statement that *Presser* "suggested that. . . nothing in the Constitution protected the use of arms outside the context of a militia," *post*, at 40, is simply wrong.

---

is wrong. It is true it was the indictment that described the right as "bearing arms for a lawful purpose." But, in explicit reference to the right described in the indictment, the Court stated that "The second amendment declares that it [*i.e.*, the right of bearing arms for a lawful purpose] shall not be infringed." 92 U. S., at 553.

[23]With respect to *Cruikshank*'s continuing validity on incorporation, a question not presented by this case, we note that *Cruikshank* also said that the First Amendment did not apply against the States and did not engage in the sort of Fourteenth Amendment inquiry required by our later cases. Our later decisions in *Presser* v. *Illinois*, 116 U. S. 252, 265 (1886) and *Miller* v. *Texas*, 153 U. S. 535, 538 (1894), reaffirmed that the Second Amendment applies only to the Federal Government.

Presser said nothing about the Second Amendment's meaning or scope, beyond the fact that it does not prevent the prohibition of private paramilitary organizations.

JUSTICE STEVENS places overwhelming reliance upon this Court's decision in *United States* v. *Miller*, 307 U. S. 174 (1939). "[H]undreds of judges," we are told, "have relied on the view of the amendment we endorsed there," *post*, at 2, and "[e]ven if the textual and historical arguments on both sides of the issue were evenly balanced, respect for the well-settled views of all of our predecessors on this Court, and for the rule of law itself . . . would prevent most jurists from endorsing such a dramatic upheaval in the law," *post*, at 4. And what is, according to JUSTICE STEVENS, the holding of *Miller* that demands such obeisance? That the Second Amendment "protects the right to keep and bear arms for certain military purposes, but that it does not curtail the legislature's power to regulate the nonmilitary use and ownership of weapons." *Post*, at 2.

Nothing so clearly demonstrates the weakness of JUSTICE STEVENS' case. *Miller* did not hold that and cannot possibly be read to have held that. The judgment in the case upheld against a Second Amendment challenge two men's federal indictment for transporting an unregistered short-barreled shotgun in interstate commerce, in violation of the National Firearms Act, 48 Stat. 1236. It is entirely clear that the Court's basis for saying that the Second Amendment did not apply was *not* that the defendants were "bear[ing] arms" not "for . . . military purposes" but for "nonmilitary use," *post*, at 2. Rather, it was that the *type of weapon at issue* was not eligible for Second Amendment protection: "In the absence of any evidence tending to show that the possession or use of a [short-barreled shotgun] at this time has some reasonable relationship to the preservation or efficiency of a well regulated militia, we cannot say that the Second Amendment guarantees the right to keep and bear *such an instrument.*" 307 U. S., at 178 (emphasis added). "Certainly," the Court continued, "it is not within judicial notice that this weapon is any part of the ordinary military equipment or that its use could contribute to the common defense." *Ibid.* Beyond that, the opinion provided no explanation of the content of the right.

This holding is not only consistent with, but positively suggests, that the Second Amendment confers an individual right to keep and bear arms (though only arms that "have some reasonable relationship to the preservation or efficiency of a well regulated militia"). Had the Court believed that the Second Amendment protects only those serving in the militia, it would have been odd to examine the character of the weapon rather than simply note that the two crooks were not militiamen. JUSTICE STEVENS can say again and again that *Miller* did "not turn on the difference between muskets and sawed-off shotguns, it turned, rather, on the basic difference between the military and nonmilitary use and possession of guns," *post*, at 42–43, but the words of the opinion prove otherwise. The most JUSTICE STEVENS can plausibly claim for *Miller* is that it declined to decide the nature of the Second Amendment right, despite the Solicitor General's argument (made in the alternative) that the right was collective, see Brief for United States, O. T. 1938, No. 696, pp. 4–5. *Miller* stands only for the proposition that the Second Amendment right, whatever its nature, extends only to certain types of weapons.

It is particularly wrongheaded to read *Miller* for more than what it said, because the case did not even purport to be a thorough examination of the Second Amendment. JUSTICE STEVENS claims, *post*, at 42, that the opinion reached its conclusion "[a]fter reviewing many of the same sources that are discussed at greater length by the Court today." Not many, which was not entirely the Court's fault. The defendants made no appearance in the case, neither filing a brief nor appearing at oral argument; the Court heard from no one but the Government (reason enough, one would think, not to make that case the beginning and the end of this Court's consideration of the Second Amendment). See Frye, The Peculiar Story of *United States* v. *Miller*, 3 N. Y. U. J. L. & Liberty 48, 65–68 (2008). The Government's brief spent two pages discussing English legal sources, concluding "that at least the carrying of weapons without lawful occasion or excuse was always a crime" and that (because of the class-based restrictions and the prohibition on terrorizing people with dangerous or unusual weapons) "the early English law did not guarantee an unrestricted right to bear arms." Brief for United States, O. T. 1938, No. 696, at 9–11. It then went on to rely primarily on the discussion of the English right to bear arms in *Aymette* v. *State*, 21 Tenn. 154, for the proposition that the only uses of arms protected by the Second Amendment are those that relate to the militia, not self-defense. See Brief for United States, O. T. 1938, No. 696, at 12–18. The final section of the brief recognized that "some courts have said that the right to bear arms includes the right of the individual to have them for the protection of his person and property," and launched an alternative argument that "weapons which are commonly used by criminals," such as sawed-off shotguns, are not protected. See *id.*, at 18–21. The Government's *Miller* brief thus provided scant discussion of the history of the Second Amendment—and the Court was presented with no counterdiscussion. As for the text of the Court's opinion itself, that discusses *none* of the history of the Second Amendment. It assumes from the prologue that the Amendment was designed to preserve the militia, 307 U. S., at 178 (which we do not dispute), and then reviews some historical materials dealing with the nature of the militia, and in particular with the nature of the arms their members were expected to possess, *id.*, at 178–182. Not a word *(not a word)* about the history of the Second Amendment. This is the mighty rock upon which the dissent rests its case.[24]

We may as well consider at this point (for we will have to consider eventually) *what* types of weapons *Miller* permits. Read in isolation, *Miller*'s phrase "part of ordinary military equipment" could mean that only those weapons useful in warfare are protected. That would be a startling reading of the opinion, since it would mean that the National Firearms Act's restrictions on machineguns (not challenged in *Miller*) might be unconstitutional, machineguns being useful in warfare in 1939. We think that *Miller*'s "ordinary military equipment" language must be read in tandem with what comes after: "[O]rdinarily when called for [militia] service [able-bodied] men were expected to appear bearing arms supplied by themselves and of the kind in common use at the time." 307 U. S., at 179. The traditional militia was formed from a pool of men bringing arms "in common use at the time" for lawful purposes like self-defense. "In the colonial and revolutionary war era, [small-arms] weapons used by militiamen and weapons used in defense of person and home were one and the same." *State* v. *Kessler*, 289 Ore. 359, 368, 614 P. 2d 94, 98 (1980) (citing G. Neumann, Swords and Blades of the American Revolution 6–15, 252–254 (1973)). Indeed, that is precisely the way in which the Second

---

[24] As for the "hundreds of judges," *post*, at 2, who have relied on the view of the Second Amendment JUSTICE STEVENS claims we endorsed in *Miller*: If so, they overread *Miller*. And their erroneous reliance upon an uncontested and virtually unreasoned case cannot nullify the reliance of millions of Americans (as our historical analysis has shown) upon the true meaning of the right to keep and bear arms. In any event, it should not be thought that the cases decided by these judges would necessarily have come out differently under a proper interpretation of the right.

Amendment's operative clause furthers the purpose announced in its preface. We therefore read *Miller* to say only that the Second Amendment does not protect those weapons not typically possessed by law-abiding citizens for lawful purposes, such as short-barreled shotguns. That accords with the historical understanding of the scope of the right, see Part III, *infra*.[25]

We conclude that nothing in our precedents forecloses our adoption of the original understanding of the Second Amendment. It should be unsurprising that such a significant matter has been for so long judicially unresolved. For most of our history, the Bill of Rights was not thought applicable to the States, and the Federal Government did not significantly regulate the possession of firearms by law-abiding citizens. Other provisions of the Bill of Rights have similarly remained unilluminated for lengthy periods. This Court first held a law to violate the First Amendment's guarantee of freedom of speech in 1931, almost 150 years after the Amendment was ratified, see *Near* v. *Minnesota ex rel. Olson*, 283 U. S. 697 (1931), and it was not until after World War II that we held a law

---

[25]*Miller* was briefly mentioned in our decision in *Lewis* v. *United States*, 445 U. S. 55 (1980), an appeal from a conviction for being a felon in possession of a firearm. The challenge was based on the contention that the prior felony conviction had been unconstitutional. No Second Amendment claim was raised or briefed by any party. In the course of rejecting the asserted challenge, the Court commented gratuitously, in a footnote, that "[t]hese legislative restrictions on the use of firearms are neither based upon constitutionally suspect criteria, nor do they trench upon any constitutionally protected liberties. See *United States* v. *Miller* . . . (the Second Amendment guarantees no right to keep and bear a firearm that does not have 'some reasonable relationship to the preservation or efficiency of a well regulated militia')." *Id.*, at 65–66, n. 8. The footnote then cites several Court of Appeals cases to the same effect. It is inconceivable that we would rest our interpretation of the basic meaning of any guarantee of the Bill of Rights upon such a footnoted dictum in a case where the point was not at issue and was not argued.

invalid under the Establishment Clause, see *Illinois ex rel. McCollum* v. *Board of Ed. of School Dist. No. 71, Champaign Cty.*, 333 U. S. 203 (1948). Even a question as basic as the scope of proscribable libel was not addressed by this Court until 1964, nearly two centuries after the founding. See *New York Times Co.* v. *Sullivan,* 376 U. S. 254 (1964). It is demonstrably not true that, as JUSTICE STEVENS claims, *post*, at 41–42, "for most of our history, the invalidity of Second-Amendment-based objections to firearms regulations has been well settled and uncontroversial." For most of our history the question did not present itself.

III

Like most rights, the right secured by the Second Amendment is not unlimited. From Blackstone through the 19th-century cases, commentators and courts routinely explained that the right was not a right to keep and carry any weapon whatsoever in any manner whatsoever and for whatever purpose. See, *e.g., Sheldon*, in 5 Blume 346; Rawle 123; Pomeroy 152–153; Abbott 333. For example, the majority of the 19th-century courts to consider the question held that prohibitions on carrying concealed weapons were lawful under the Second Amendment or state analogues. See, *e.g., State* v. *Chandler*, 5 La. Ann., at 489–490; *Nunn* v. *State*, 1 Ga., at 251; see generally 2 Kent *340, n. 2; The American Students' Blackstone 84, n. 11 (G. Chase ed. 1884). Although we do not undertake an exhaustive historical analysis today of the full scope of the Second Amendment, nothing in our opinion should be taken to cast doubt on longstanding prohibitions on the possession of firearms by felons and the mentally ill, or laws forbidding the carrying of firearms in sensitive places such as schools and government buildings, or laws imposing conditions and qualifications on the commercial sale of

Opinion of the Court

arms.[26]

We also recognize another important limitation on the right to keep and carry arms. *Miller* said, as we have explained, that the sorts of weapons protected were those "in common use at the time." 307 U. S., at 179. We think that limitation is fairly supported by the historical tradition of prohibiting the carrying of "dangerous and unusual weapons." See 4 Blackstone 148–149 (1769); 3 B. Wilson, Works of the Honourable James Wilson 79 (1804); J. Dunlap, The New-York Justice 8 (1815); C. Humphreys, A Compendium of the Common Law in Force in Kentucky 482 (1822); 1 W. Russell, A Treatise on Crimes and Indictable Misdemeanors 271–272 (1831); H. Stephen, Summary of the Criminal Law 48 (1840); E. Lewis, An Abridgment of the Criminal Law of the United States 64 (1847); F. Wharton, A Treatise on the Criminal Law of the United States 726 (1852). See also *State* v. *Langford*, 10 N. C. 381, 383–384 (1824); *O'Neill* v. *State*, 16 Ala. 65, 67 (1849); *English* v. *State*, 35 Tex. 473, 476 (1871); *State* v. *Lanier*, 71 N. C. 288, 289 (1874).

It may be objected that if weapons that are most useful in military service—M-16 rifles and the like—may be banned, then the Second Amendment right is completely detached from the prefatory clause. But as we have said, the conception of the militia at the time of the Second Amendment's ratification was the body of all citizens capable of military service, who would bring the sorts of lawful weapons that they possessed at home to militia duty. It may well be true today that a militia, to be as effective as militias in the 18th century, would require sophisticated arms that are highly unusual in society at large. Indeed, it may be true that no amount of small arms could be useful against modern-day bombers and

---

[26] We identify these presumptively lawful regulatory measures only as examples; our list does not purport to be exhaustive.

tanks. But the fact that modern developments have limited the degree of fit between the prefatory clause and the protected right cannot change our interpretation of the right.

IV

We turn finally to the law at issue here. As we have said, the law totally bans handgun possession in the home. It also requires that any lawful firearm in the home be disassembled or bound by a trigger lock at all times, rendering it inoperable.

As the quotations earlier in this opinion demonstrate, the inherent right of self-defense has been central to the Second Amendment right. The handgun ban amounts to a prohibition of an entire class of "arms" that is overwhelmingly chosen by American society for that lawful purpose. The prohibition extends, moreover, to the home, where the need for defense of self, family, and property is most acute. Under any of the standards of scrutiny that we have applied to enumerated constitutional rights,[27] banning from

---

[27] JUSTICE BREYER correctly notes that this law, like almost all laws, would pass rational-basis scrutiny. *Post*, at 8. But rational-basis scrutiny is a mode of analysis we have used when evaluating laws under constitutional commands that are themselves prohibitions on irrational laws. See, *e.g.*, *Engquist* v. *Oregon Dept. of Agriculture*, 553 U. S. ___, ___ (2008) (slip op., at 9–10). In those cases, "rational basis" is not just the standard of scrutiny, but the very substance of the constitutional guarantee. Obviously, the same test could not be used to evaluate the extent to which a legislature may regulate a specific, enumerated right, be it the freedom of speech, the guarantee against double jeopardy, the right to counsel, or the right to keep and bear arms. See *United States* v. *Carolene Products Co.*, 304 U. S. 144, 152, n. 4 (1938) ("There may be narrower scope for operation of the presumption of constitutionality [*i.e.*, narrower than that provided by rational-basis review] when legislation appears on its face to be within a specific prohibition of the Constitution, such as those of the first ten amendments. . ."). If all that was required to overcome the right to keep and bear arms was a rational basis, the Second Amendment would be redundant with the separate constitutional prohibitions on irra-

Opinion of the Court

the home "the most preferred firearm in the nation to 'keep' and use for protection of one's home and family," 478 F. 3d, at 400, would fail constitutional muster.

Few laws in the history of our Nation have come close to the severe restriction of the District's handgun ban. And some of those few have been struck down. In *Nunn* v. *State*, the Georgia Supreme Court struck down a prohibition on carrying pistols openly (even though it upheld a prohibition on carrying concealed weapons). See 1 Ga., at 251. In *Andrews* v. *State*, the Tennessee Supreme Court likewise held that a statute that forbade openly carrying a pistol "publicly or privately, without regard to time or place, or circumstances," 50 Tenn., at 187, violated the state constitutional provision (which the court equated with the Second Amendment). That was so even though the statute did not restrict the carrying of long guns. *Ibid.* See also *State* v. *Reid*, 1 Ala. 612, 616–617 (1840) ("A statute which, under the pretence of regulating, amounts to a destruction of the right, or which requires arms to be so borne as to render them wholly useless for the purpose of defence, would be clearly unconstitutional").

It is no answer to say, as petitioners do, that it is permissible to ban the possession of handguns so long as the possession of other firearms (*i.e.*, long guns) is allowed. It is enough to note, as we have observed, that the American people have considered the handgun to be the quintessential self-defense weapon. There are many reasons that a citizen may prefer a handgun for home defense: It is easier to store in a location that is readily accessible in an emergency; it cannot easily be redirected or wrestled away by an attacker; it is easier to use for those without the upper-body strength to lift and aim a long gun; it can be pointed at a burglar with one hand while the other hand dials the police. Whatever the reason, handguns are the most popu-

─────────

tional laws, and would have no effect.

lar weapon chosen by Americans for self-defense in the home, and a complete prohibition of their use is invalid.

We must also address the District's requirement (as applied to respondent's handgun) that firearms in the home be rendered and kept inoperable at all times. This makes it impossible for citizens to use them for the core lawful purpose of self-defense and is hence unconstitutional. The District argues that we should interpret this element of the statute to contain an exception for self-defense. See Brief for Petitioners 56–57. But we think that is precluded by the unequivocal text, and by the presence of certain other enumerated exceptions: "Except for law enforcement personnel . . . , each registrant shall keep any firearm in his possession unloaded and disassembled or bound by a trigger lock or similar device unless such firearm is kept at his place of business, or while being used for lawful recreational purposes within the District of Columbia." D. C. Code §7–2507.02. The nonexistence of a self-defense exception is also suggested by the D. C. Court of Appeals' statement that the statute forbids residents to use firearms to stop intruders, see *McIntosh* v. *Washington*, 395 A. 2d 744, 755–756 (1978).[28]

Apart from his challenge to the handgun ban and the trigger-lock requirement respondent asked the District Court to enjoin petitioners from enforcing the separate licensing requirement "in such a manner as to forbid the carrying of a firearm within one's home or possessed land without a license." App. 59a. The Court of Appeals did not invalidate the licensing requirement, but held only

---

[28] *McIntosh* upheld the law against a claim that it violated the Equal Protection Clause by arbitrarily distinguishing between residences and businesses. See 395 A. 2d, at 755. One of the rational bases listed for that distinction was the legislative finding "that for each intruder stopped by a firearm there are four gun-related accidents within the home." *Ibid.* That tradeoff would not bear mention if the statute did not prevent stopping intruders by firearms.

that the District "may not prevent [a handgun] from being moved throughout one's house." 478 F. 3d, at 400. It then ordered the District Court to enter summary judgment "consistent with [respondent's] prayer for relief." *Id.*, at 401. Before this Court petitioners have stated that "if the handgun ban is struck down and respondent registers a handgun, he could obtain a license, assuming he is not otherwise disqualified," by which they apparently mean if he is not a felon and is not insane. Brief for Petitioners 58. Respondent conceded at oral argument that he does not "have a problem with . . . licensing" and that the District's law is permissible so long as it is "not enforced in an arbitrary and capricious manner." Tr. of Oral Arg. 74–75. We therefore assume that petitioners' issuance of a license will satisfy respondent's prayer for relief and do not address the licensing requirement.

JUSTICE BREYER has devoted most of his separate dissent to the handgun ban. He says that, even assuming the Second Amendment is a personal guarantee of the right to bear arms, the District's prohibition is valid. He first tries to establish this by founding-era historical precedent, pointing to various restrictive laws in the colonial period. These demonstrate, in his view, that the District's law "imposes a burden upon gun owners that seems proportionately no greater than restrictions in existence at the time the Second Amendment was adopted." *Post*, at 2. Of the laws he cites, only one offers even marginal support for his assertion. A 1783 Massachusetts law forbade the residents of Boston to "take into" or "receive into" "any Dwelling House, Stable, Barn, Out-house, Ware-house, Store, Shop or other Building" loaded firearms, and permitted the seizure of any loaded firearms that "shall be found" there. Act of Mar. 1, 1783, ch. 13, 1783 Mass. Acts p. 218. That statute's text and its prologue, which makes clear that the purpose of the prohibition was to eliminate the danger to firefighters posed by the "depositing of loaded Arms" in buildings, give reason to doubt that colonial Boston authorities would have enforced that general prohibition against someone who temporarily loaded a firearm to confront an intruder (despite the law's application in that case). In any case, we would not stake our interpretation of the Second Amendment upon a single law, in effect in a single city, that contradicts the overwhelming weight of other evidence regarding the right to keep and bear arms for defense of the home. The other laws JUSTICE BREYER cites are gunpowder-storage laws that he concedes did not clearly prohibit loaded weapons, but required only that excess gunpowder be kept in a special container or on the top floor of the home. *Post*, at 6–7. Nothing about those fire-safety laws undermines our analysis; they do not remotely burden the right of self-defense as much as an absolute ban on handguns. Nor, correspondingly, does our analysis suggest the invalidity of laws regulating the storage of firearms to prevent accidents.

JUSTICE BREYER points to other founding-era laws that he says "restricted the firing of guns within the city limits to at least some degree" in Boston, Philadelphia and New York. *Post*, at 4 (citing Churchill, Gun Regulation, the Police Power, and the Right to Keep Arms in Early America, 25 Law & Hist. Rev. 139, 162 (2007)). Those laws provide no support for the severe restriction in the present case. The New York law levied a fine of 20 shillings on anyone who fired a gun in certain places (including houses) on New Year's Eve and the first two days of January, and was aimed at preventing the "great Damages . . . frequently done on [those days] by persons going House to House, with Guns and other Firearms and being often intoxicated with Liquor." 5 Colonial Laws of New York 244–246 (1894). It is inconceivable that this law would have been enforced against a person exercising his right to self-defense on New Year's Day against such drunken hooligans.   The Pennsylvania law to which JUSTICE BREYER refers levied a fine of 5 shillings on one who fired a gun or set off fireworks in Philadelphia without first obtaining a license from the governor. See Act of Aug. 26, 1721, §4, in 3 Stat. at Large 253–254. Given Justice Wilson's explanation that the right to self-defense with arms was protected by the Pennsylvania Constitution, it is unlikely that this law (which in any event amounted to at most a licensing regime) would have been enforced against a person who used firearms for self-defense.   JUSTICE BREYER cites a Rhode Island law that simply levied a 5-shilling fine on those who fired guns in *streets* and *taverns*, a law obviously inapplicable to this case. See An Act for preventing Mischief being done in the town of Newport, or in any other town in this Government, 1731, Rhode Island Session Laws. Finally, JUSTICE BREYER points to a Massachusetts law similar to the Pennsylvania law, prohibiting "discharg[ing] any Gun or Pistol charged with Shot or Ball in the Town of *Boston*." Act of May 28, 1746, ch. X, Acts and Laws of Mass. Bay 208. It is again implausible that this would have been enforced against a citizen acting in self-defense, particularly given its preambulatory reference to "the *indiscreet* firing of Guns." *Ibid.* (preamble) (emphasis added).

A broader point about the laws that JUSTICE BREYER cites: All of them punished the discharge (or loading) of guns with a small fine and forfeiture of the weapon (or in a few cases a very brief stay in the local jail), not with significant criminal penalties.[29]   They are akin to modern penalties for minor public-safety infractions like speeding

---

[29] The Supreme Court of Pennsylvania described the amount of five shillings in a contract matter in 1792 as "nominal consideration." *Morris's Lessee* v. *Smith*, 4 Dall. 119, 120 (Pa. 1792). Many of the laws cited punished violation with fine in a similar amount; the 1783 Massachusetts gunpowder-storage law carried a somewhat larger fine of £10 (200 shillings) and forfeiture of the weapon.

or jaywalking. And although such public-safety laws may not contain exceptions for self-defense, it is inconceivable that the threat of a jaywalking ticket would deter someone from disregarding a "Do Not Walk" sign in order to flee an attacker, or that the Government would enforce those laws under such circumstances. Likewise, we do not think that a law imposing a 5-shilling fine and forfeiture of the gun would have prevented a person in the founding era from using a gun to protect himself or his family from violence, or that if he did so the law would be enforced against him. The District law, by contrast, far from imposing a minor fine, threatens citizens with a year in prison (five years for a second violation) for even obtaining a gun in the first place. See D. C. Code §7–2507.06.

JUSTICE BREYER moves on to make a broad jurisprudential point: He criticizes us for declining to establish a level of scrutiny for evaluating Second Amendment restrictions. He proposes, explicitly at least, none of the traditionally expressed levels (strict scrutiny, intermediate scrutiny, rational basis), but rather a judge-empowering "interest-balancing inquiry" that "asks whether the statute burdens a protected interest in a way or to an extent that is out of proportion to the statute's salutary effects upon other important governmental interests." *Post*, at 10. After an exhaustive discussion of the arguments for and against gun control, JUSTICE BREYER arrives at his interest-balanced answer: because handgun violence is a problem, because the law is limited to an urban area, and because there were somewhat similar restrictions in the founding period (a false proposition that we have already discussed), the interest-balancing inquiry results in the constitutionality of the handgun ban. QED.

We know of no other enumerated constitutional right whose core protection has been subjected to a freestanding "interest-balancing" approach. The very enumeration of the right takes out of the hands of government—even the

Third Branch of Government—the power to decide on a case-by-case basis whether the right is *really worth* insisting upon. A constitutional guarantee subject to future judges' assessments of its usefulness is no constitutional guarantee at all. Constitutional rights are enshrined with the scope they were understood to have when the people adopted them, whether or not future legislatures or (yes) even future judges think that scope too broad. We would not apply an "interest-balancing" approach to the prohibition of a peaceful neo-Nazi march through Skokie. See *National Socialist Party of America* v. *Skokie*, 432 U. S. 43 (1977) *(per curiam)*. The First Amendment contains the freedom-of-speech guarantee that the people ratified, which included exceptions for obscenity, libel, and disclosure of state secrets, but not for the expression of extremely unpopular and wrong-headed views. The Second Amendment is no different. Like the First, it is the very *product* of an interest-balancing by the people—which JUSTICE BREYER would now conduct for them anew. And whatever else it leaves to future evaluation, it surely elevates above all other interests the right of law-abiding, responsible citizens to use arms in defense of hearth and home.

JUSTICE BREYER chides us for leaving so many applications of the right to keep and bear arms in doubt, and for not providing extensive historical justification for those regulations of the right that we describe as permissible. See *post*, at 42–43. But since this case represents this Court's first in-depth examination of the Second Amendment, one should not expect it to clarify the entire field, any more than *Reynolds* v. *United States*, 98 U. S. 145 (1879), our first in-depth Free Exercise Clause case, left that area in a state of utter certainty. And there will be time enough to expound upon the historical justifications for the exceptions we have mentioned if and when those exceptions come before us.

In sum, we hold that the District's ban on handgun possession in the home violates the Second Amendment, as does its prohibition against rendering any lawful firearm in the home operable for the purpose of immediate self-defense. Assuming that Heller is not disqualified from the exercise of Second Amendment rights, the District must permit him to register his handgun and must issue him a license to carry it in the home.

* * *

We are aware of the problem of handgun violence in this country, and we take seriously the concerns raised by the many *amici* who believe that prohibition of handgun ownership is a solution. The Constitution leaves the District of Columbia a variety of tools for combating that problem, including some measures regulating handguns, see *supra,* at 54–55, and n. 26. But the enshrinement of constitutional rights necessarily takes certain policy choices off the table. These include the absolute prohibition of handguns held and used for self-defense in the home. Undoubtedly some think that the Second Amendment is outmoded in a society where our standing army is the pride of our Nation, where well-trained police forces provide personal security, and where gun violence is a serious problem. That is perhaps debatable, but what is not debatable is that it is not the role of this Court to pronounce the Second Amendment extinct.

We affirm the judgment of the Court of Appeals.

It is so ordered.

SUPREME COURT OF THE UNITED STATES

No. 07–290

DISTRICT OF COLUMBIA, ET AL., PETITIONERS *v.*
DICK ANTHONY HELLER

ON WRIT OF CERTIORARI TO THE UNITED STATES COURT OF
APPEALS FOR THE DISTRICT OF COLUMBIA CIRCUIT

[June 26, 2008]

JUSTICE STEVENS, with whom JUSTICE SOUTER, JUSTICE GINSBURG, and JUSTICE BREYER join, dissenting.

The question presented by this case is not whether the Second Amendment protects a "collective right" or an "individual right." Surely it protects a right that can be enforced by individuals. But a conclusion that the Second Amendment protects an individual right does not tell us anything about the scope of that right.

Guns are used to hunt, for self-defense, to commit crimes, for sporting activities, and to perform military duties. The Second Amendment plainly does not protect the right to use a gun to rob a bank; it is equally clear that it *does* encompass the right to use weapons for certain military purposes. Whether it also protects the right to possess and use guns for nonmilitary purposes like hunting and personal self-defense is the question presented by this case. The text of the Amendment, its history, and our decision in *United States* v. *Miller*, 307 U. S. 174 (1939), provide a clear answer to that question.

The Second Amendment was adopted to protect the right of the people of each of the several States to maintain a well-regulated militia. It was a response to concerns raised during the ratification of the Constitution that the power of Congress to disarm the state militias and create a national standing army posed an intolerable threat to the sovereignty of the several States. Neither the text of the Amendment nor the arguments advanced by its proponents evidenced the slightest interest in limiting any legislature's authority to regulate private civilian uses of firearms. Specifically, there is no indication that the Framers of the Amendment intended to enshrine the common-law right of self-defense in the Constitution.

In 1934, Congress enacted the National Firearms Act, the first major federal firearms law.[1] Sustaining an indictment under the Act, this Court held that, "[i]n the absence of any evidence tending to show that possession or use of a 'shotgun having a barrel of less than eighteen inches in length' at this time has some reasonable relationship to the preservation or efficiency of a well regulated militia, we cannot say that the Second Amendment guarantees the right to keep and bear such an instrument." *Miller*, 307 U. S., at 178. The view of the Amendment we took in *Miller*—that it protects the right to keep and bear arms for certain military purposes, but that it does not curtail the Legislature's power to regulate the nonmilitary use and ownership of weapons—is both the most natural reading of the Amendment's text and the interpretation most faithful to the history of its adoption.

Since our decision in *Miller,* hundreds of judges have relied on the view of the Amendment we endorsed there;[2]

---

[1] There was some limited congressional activity earlier: A 10% federal excise tax on firearms was passed as part of the Revenue Act of 1918, 40 Stat. 1057, and in 1927 a statute was enacted prohibiting the shipment of handguns, revolvers, and other concealable weapons through the United States mails. Ch. 75, 44 Stat. 1059–1060 (hereinafter 1927 Act).

[2] Until the Fifth Circuit's decision in *United States* v. *Emerson*, 270 F. 3d 203 (2001), every Court of Appeals to consider the question had understood *Miller* to hold that the Second Amendment does not protect the right to possess and use guns for purely private, civilian purposes. See, *e.g., United States* v. *Haney,* 264 F. 3d 1161, 1164–1166 (CA10 2001); *United States* v. *Napier,* 233 F. 3d 394, 402–404 (CA6 2000);

we ourselves affirmed it in 1980. See *Lewis* v. *United States,* 445 U. S. 55, 65–66, n. 8 (1980).[3] No new evidence has surfaced since 1980 supporting the view that the Amendment was intended to curtail the power of Congress to regulate civilian use or misuse of weapons. Indeed, a review of the drafting history of the Amendment demonstrates that its Framers *rejected* proposals that would have broadened its coverage to include such uses.

The opinion the Court announces today fails to identify any new evidence supporting the view that the Amendment was intended to limit the power of Congress to regulate civilian uses of weapons. Unable to point to any such evidence, the Court stakes its holding on a strained and

---

Gillespie v. *Indianapolis,* 185 F. 3d 693, 710–711 (CA7 1999); *United States* v. *Scanio,* No. 97–1584, 1998 WL 802060, *2 (CA2, Nov. 12, 1998) (unpublished opinion); *United States* v. *Wright,* 117 F. 3d 1265, 1271–1274 (CA11 1997); *United States* v. *Rybar,* 103 F. 3d 273, 285–286 (CA3 1996); *Hickman* v. *Block,* 81 F. 3d 98, 100–103 (CA9 1996); *United States* v. *Hale,* 978 F. 2d 1016, 1018–1020 (CA8 1992); *Thomas* v. *City Council of Portland,* 730 F. 2d 41, 42 (CA1 1984) *(per curiam); United States* v. *Johnson,* 497 F. 2d 548, 550 (CA4 1974) *(per curiam); United States* v. *Johnson,* 441 F. 2d 1134, 1136 (CA5 1971); see also *Sandidge* v. *United States,* 520 A. 2d 1057, 1058–1059 (DC App. 1987). And a number of courts have remained firm in their prior positions, even after considering *Emerson.* See, *e.g., United States* v. *Lippman,* 369 F. 3d 1039, 1043–1045 (CA8 2004); *United States* v. *Parker,* 362 F. 3d 1279, 1282–1284 (CA10 2004); *United States* v. *Jackubowski,* 63 Fed. Appx. 959, 961 (CA7 2003) (unpublished opinion); *Silveira* v. *Lockyer,* 312 F. 3d 1052, 1060–1066 (CA9 2002); *United States* v. *Milheron,* 231 F. Supp. 2d 376, 378 (Me. 2002); *Bach* v. *Pataki,* 289 F. Supp. 2d 217, 224–226 (NDNY 2003); *United States* v. *Smith,* 56 M. J. 711, 716 (C. A. Armed Forces 2001).

[3] Our discussion in *Lewis* was brief but significant. Upholding a conviction for receipt of a firearm by a felon, we wrote: "These legislative restrictions on the use of firearms are neither based upon constitutionally suspect criteria, nor do they entrench upon any constitutionally protected liberties. See *United States* v. *Miller,* 307 U. S. 174, 178 (1939) (the Second Amendment guarantees no right to keep and bear a firearm that does not have 'some reasonable relationship to the preservation or efficiency of a well regulated militia')." 445 U. S., at 65, n. 8.

unpersuasive reading of the Amendment's text; significantly different provisions in the 1689 English Bill of Rights, and in various 19th-century State Constitutions; postenactment commentary that was available to the Court when it decided *Miller;* and, ultimately, a feeble attempt to distinguish *Miller* that places more emphasis on the Court's decisional process than on the reasoning in the opinion itself.

Even if the textual and historical arguments on both sides of the issue were evenly balanced, respect for the well-settled views of all of our predecessors on this Court, and for the rule of law itself, see *Mitchell* v. *W. T. Grant Co.,* 416 U. S. 600, 636 (1974) (Stewart, J., dissenting), would prevent most jurists from endorsing such a dramatic upheaval in the law.[4] As Justice Cardozo observed years ago, the "labor of judges would be increased almost to the breaking point if every past decision could be reopened in every case, and one could not lay one's own

---

[4] See *Vasquez* v. *Hillery,* 474 U. S. 254, 265, 266 (1986) ("*[Stare decisis]* permits society to presume that bedrock principles are founded in the law rather than in the proclivities of individuals, and thereby contributes to the integrity of our constitutional system of government, both in appearance and in fact. While *stare decisis* is not an inexorable command, the careful observer will discern that any detours from the straight path of *stare decisis* in our past have occurred for articulable reasons, and only when the Court has felt obliged 'to bring its opinions into agreement with experience and with facts newly ascertained.' *Burnet* v. *Coronado Oil & Gas Co.,* 285 U. S. 393, 412 (1932) (Brandeis, J., dissenting)"); *Pollock* v. *Farmers' Loan & Trust Co.,* 157 U. S. 429, 652 (1895) (White, J., dissenting) ("The fundamental conception of a judicial body is that of one hedged about by precedents which are binding on the court without regard to the personality of its members. Break down this belief in judicial continuity and let it be felt that on great constitutional questions this Court is to depart from the settled conclusions of its predecessors, and to determine them all according to the mere opinion of those who temporarily fill its bench, and our Constitution will, in my judgment, be bereft of value and become a most dangerous instrument to the rights and liberties of the people").

course of bricks on the secure foundation of the courses laid by others who had gone before him." The Nature of the Judicial Process 149 (1921).

In this dissent I shall first explain why our decision in *Miller* was faithful to the text of the Second Amendment and the purposes revealed in its drafting history. I shall then comment on the postratification history of the Amendment, which makes abundantly clear that the Amendment should not be interpreted as limiting the authority of Congress to regulate the use or possession of firearms for purely civilian purposes.

I

The text of the Second Amendment is brief. It provides: "A well regulated Militia, being necessary to the security of a free State, the right of the people to keep and bear Arms, shall not be infringed."

Three portions of that text merit special focus: the introductory language defining the Amendment's purpose, the class of persons encompassed within its reach, and the unitary nature of the right that it protects.

"A well regulated Militia, being necessary to the security of a free State"

The preamble to the Second Amendment makes three important points. It identifies the preservation of the militia as the Amendment's purpose; it explains that the militia is necessary to the security of a free State; and it recognizes that the militia must be "well regulated." In all three respects it is comparable to provisions in several State Declarations of Rights that were adopted roughly contemporaneously with the Declaration of Independence.[5]

---

[5] The Virginia Declaration of Rights ¶13 (1776), provided: "That a well-regulated militia, composed of the body of the people, trained to arms, is the proper, natural, and safe defence of a free State; that Standing Armies, in time of peace, should be avoided, as dangerous to

Those state provisions highlight the importance members
of the founding generation attached to the maintenance of
state militias; they also underscore the profound fear
shared by many in that era of the dangers posed by standing armies.[6] While the need for state militias has not been

---

liberty; and that, in all cases, the military should be under strict
subordination to, and governed by, the civil power." 1 B. Schwartz, The
Bill of Rights 235 (1971) (hereinafter Schwartz).

Maryland's Declaration of Rights, Arts. XXV–XXVII (1776), provided:
"That a well-regulated militia is the proper and natural defence of a
free government"; "That standing armies are dangerous to liberty, and
ought not to be raised or kept up, without consent of the Legislature";
"That in all cases, and at all times, the military ought to be under strict
subordination to and control of the civil power." 1 Schwartz 282.

Delaware's Declaration of Rights, §§18–20 (1776), provided: "That a
well regulated militia is the proper, natural, and safe defence of a free
government"; "That standing armies are dangerous to liberty, and
ought not to be raised or kept up without the consent of the Legislature"; "That in all cases and at all times the military ought to be under
strict subordination to and governed by the civil power." 1 Schwartz
278.

Finally, New Hampshire's Bill of Rights, Arts. XXIV–XXVI (1783),
read: "A well regulated militia is the proper, natural, and sure defence
of a state"; "Standing armies are dangerous to liberty, and ought not to
be raised or kept up without consent of the legislature"; "In all cases,
and at all times, the military ought to be under strict subordination to,
and governed by the civil power." 1 Schwartz 378. It elsewhere provided: "No person who is conscientiously scrupulous about the lawful-
ness of bearing arms, shall be compelled thereto, provided he will pay
an equivalent." *Id.,* at 377 (Art. XIII).

[6] The language of the Amendment's preamble also closely tracks the
language of a number of contemporaneous state militia statutes, many
of which began with nearly identical statements. Georgia's 1778 militia
statute, for example, began, "[w]hereas a well ordered and disciplined
Militia, is essentially necessary, to the Safety, peace and prosperity, of
this State." Act of Nov. 15, 1778, 19 Colonial Records of the State of
Georgia 103 (Candler ed. 1911 (pt. 2)). North Carolina's 1777 militia
statute started with this language: "Whereas a well regulated Militia is
absolutely necessary for the defending and securing the Liberties of a
free State." N. C. Sess. Laws ch. 1, §I, p. 1. And Connecticut's 1782
"Acts and Laws Regulating the Militia" began, "Whereas the Defence

a matter of significant public interest for almost two centuries, that fact should not obscure the contemporary concerns that animated the Framers.

The parallels between the Second Amendment and these state declarations, and the Second Amendment's omission of any statement of purpose related to the right to use firearms for hunting or personal self-defense, is especially striking in light of the fact that the Declarations of Rights of Pennsylvania and Vermont *did* expressly protect such civilian uses at the time. Article XIII of Pennsylvania's 1776 Declaration of Rights announced that "the people have a right to bear arms for the defence *of themselves* and the state," 1 Schwartz 266 (emphasis added); §43 of the Declaration assured that "the inhabitants of this state shall have the liberty to fowl and hunt in seasonable times on the lands they hold, and on all other lands therein not inclosed," *id.,* at 274. And Article XV of the 1777 Vermont Declaration of Rights guaranteed "[t]hat the people have a right to bear arms for the defence *of themselves* and the State." *Id.,* at 324 (emphasis added). The contrast between those two declarations and the Second Amendment reinforces the clear statement of purpose announced in the Amendment's preamble. It

---

and Security of all free States depends (under God) upon the Exertions of a well regulated Militia, and the Laws heretofore enacted have proved inadequate to the End designed." Conn. Acts and Laws p. 585 (hereinafter 1782 Conn. Acts).

These state militia statutes give content to the notion of a "well-regulated militia." They identify those persons who compose the State's militia; they create regiments, brigades, and divisions; they set forth command structures and provide for the appointment of officers; they describe how the militia will be assembled when necessary and provide for training; and they prescribe penalties for nonappearance, delinquency, and failure to keep the required weapons, ammunition, and other necessary equipment. The obligation of militia members to "keep" certain specified arms is detailed further, n. 14, *infra,* and accompanying text.

confirms that the Framers' single-minded focus in crafting the constitutional guarantee "to keep and bear arms" was on military uses of firearms, which they viewed in the context of service in state militias.

The preamble thus both sets forth the object of the Amendment and informs the meaning of the remainder of its text. Such text should not be treated as mere surplusage, for "[i]t cannot be presumed that any clause in the constitution is intended to be without effect." *Marbury* v. *Madison,* 1 Cranch 137, 174 (1803).

The Court today tries to denigrate the importance of this clause of the Amendment by beginning its analysis with the Amendment's operative provision and returning to the preamble merely "to ensure that our reading of the operative clause is consistent with the announced purpose." *Ante,* at 5. That is not how this Court ordinarily reads such texts, and it is not how the preamble would have been viewed at the time the Amendment was adopted. While the Court makes the novel suggestion that it need only find some "logical connection" between the preamble and the operative provision, it does acknowledge that a prefatory clause may resolve an ambiguity in the text. *Ante,* at 4.[7] Without identifying any language in the

---

[7] The sources the Court cites simply do not support the proposition that some "logical connection" between the two clauses is all that is required. The Dwarris treatise, for example, merely explains that "[t]he general purview of a statute is not . . . *necessarily* to be restrained by any words introductory to the enacting clauses." F. Dwarris, A General Treatise on Statutes 268 (P. Potter ed. 1871) (emphasis added). The treatise proceeds to caution that "the preamble cannot control the enacting part of a statute, which is expressed in clear and unambiguous terms, yet, if any doubt arise on the words of the enacting part, the preamble may be resorted to, to explain it." *Id.,* at 269. Sutherland makes the same point. Explaining that "[i]n the United States preambles are not as important as they are in England," the treatise notes that in the United States "the settled principle of law is that the preamble cannot control the enacting part of the statute *in cases where the*

text that even mentions civilian uses of firearms, the Court proceeds to "find" its preferred reading in what is at best an ambiguous text, and then concludes that its reading is not foreclosed by the preamble. Perhaps the Court's approach to the text is acceptable advocacy, but it is surely an unusual approach for judges to follow.

"The right of the people"

The centerpiece of the Court's textual argument is its insistence that the words "the people" as used in the Second Amendment must have the same meaning, and protect the same class of individuals, as when they are used in the First and Fourth Amendments. According to the Court, in all three provisions—as well as the Constitution's preamble, section 2 of Article I, and the Tenth Amendment—"the term unambiguously refers to all members of the political community, not an unspecified subset." *Ante,* at 6. But the Court *itself* reads the Second Amendment to protect a "subset" significantly narrower than the class of persons protected by the First and Fourth Amendments; when it finally drills down on the substantive meaning of the Second Amendment, the Court limits the protected class to "law-abiding, responsible citizens," *ante,* at 63. But the class of persons protected by the First and Fourth Amendments is *not* so limited; for even felons (and presumably irresponsible citizens as well) may invoke the protections of those constitutional provisions. The Court offers no way to harmonize its conflicting pronouncements.

The Court also overlooks the significance of the way the

---

enacting part is expressed in clear, unambiguous terms." 2A N. Singer, Sutherland on Statutory Construction §47.04, p. 146 (rev. 5th ed. 1992) (emphasis added). Surely not even the Court believes that the Amendment's operative provision, which, though only 14 words in length, takes the Court the better part of 18 pages to parse, is perfectly "clear and unambiguous."

Framers used the phrase "the people" in these constitutional provisions. In the First Amendment, no words define the class of individuals entitled to speak, to publish, or to worship; in that Amendment it is only the right peaceably to assemble, and to petition the Government for a redress of grievances, that is described as a right of "the people." These rights contemplate collective action. While the right peaceably to assemble protects the individual rights of those persons participating in the assembly, its concern is with action engaged in by members of a group, rather than any single individual. Likewise, although the act of petitioning the Government is a right that can be exercised by individuals, it is primarily collective in nature. For if they are to be effective, petitions must involve groups of individuals acting in concert.

Similarly, the words "the people" in the Second Amendment refer back to the object announced in the Amendment's preamble. They remind us that it is the collective action of individuals having a duty to serve in the militia that the text directly protects and, perhaps more importantly, that the ultimate purpose of the Amendment was to protect the States' share of the divided sovereignty created by the Constitution.

As used in the Fourth Amendment, "the people" describes the class of persons protected from unreasonable searches and seizures by Government officials. It is true that the Fourth Amendment describes a right that need not be exercised in any collective sense. But that observation does not settle the meaning of the phrase "the people" when used in the Second Amendment. For, as we have seen, the phrase means something quite different in the Petition and Assembly Clauses of the First Amendment. Although the abstract definition of the phrase "the people" could carry the same meaning in the Second Amendment as in the Fourth Amendment, the preamble of the Second Amendment suggests that the uses of the phrase in the

First and Second Amendments are the same in referring to a collective activity. By way of contrast, the Fourth Amendment describes a right *against* governmental interference rather than an affirmative right *to* engage in protected conduct, and so refers to a right to protect a purely individual interest. As used in the Second Amendment, the words "the people" do not enlarge the right to keep and bear arms to encompass use or ownership of weapons outside the context of service in a well-regulated militia.

"To keep and bear Arms"

Although the Court's discussion of these words treats them as two "phrases"—as if they read "to keep" and "to bear"—they describe a unitary right: to possess arms if needed for military purposes and to use them in conjunction with military activities.

As a threshold matter, it is worth pausing to note an oddity in the Court's interpretation of "to keep and bear arms." Unlike the Court of Appeals, the Court does not read that phrase to create a right to possess arms for "lawful, private purposes." *Parker* v. *District of Columbia,* 478 F. 3d 370, 382 (CADC 2007). Instead, the Court limits the Amendment's protection to the right "to possess and carry weapons in case of confrontation." *Ante,* at 19. No party or *amicus* urged this interpretation; the Court appears to have fashioned it out of whole cloth. But although this novel limitation lacks support in the text of the Amendment, the Amendment's text *does* justify a different limitation: the "right to keep and bear arms" protects only a right to possess and use firearms in connection with service in a state-organized militia.

The term "bear arms" is a familiar idiom; when used unadorned by any additional words, its meaning is "to serve as a soldier, do military service, fight." 1 Oxford English Dictionary 634 (2d ed. 1989). It is derived from the Latin *arma ferre,* which, translated literally, means "to bear *[ferre]* war equipment *[arma]*." Brief for Professors of Linguistics and English as *Amici Curiae* 19. One 18th-century dictionary defined "arms" as "weapons of offence, or armour of defence," 1 S. Johnson, A Dictionary of the English Language (1755), and another contemporaneous source explained that "[b]y *arms,* we understand those instruments of offence generally made use of in war; such as firearms, swords, & c. By *weapons,* we more particularly mean instruments of other kinds (exclusive of firearms), made use of as offensive, on special occasions." 1 J. Trusler, The Distinction Between Words Esteemed Synonymous in the English Language 37 (1794).[8] Had the Framers wished to expand the meaning of the phrase "bear arms" to encompass civilian possession and use, they could have done so by the addition of phrases such as "for the defense of themselves," as was done in the Pennsylvania and Vermont Declarations of Rights. The *unmodified* use of "bear arms," by contrast, refers most naturally to a military purpose, as evidenced by its use in literally dozens of contemporary texts.[9] The absence of any refer-

---

[8] The Court's repeated citation to the dissenting opinion in *Muscarello* v. *United States,* 524 U. S. 125 (1998), *ante,* at 10, 13, as illuminating the meaning of "bear arms," borders on the risible. At issue in *Muscarello* was the proper construction of the word "carries" in 18 U. S. C. §924(c) (2000 ed. and Supp. V); the dissent in that case made passing reference to the Second Amendment only in the course of observing that both the Constitution and Black's Law Dictionary suggested that something more active than placement of a gun in a glove compartment might be meant by the phrase "'carries a firearm.'" 524 U. S., at 143.

[9] *Amici* professors of Linguistics and English reviewed uses of the term "bear arms" in a compilation of books, pamphlets, and other sources disseminated in the period between the Declaration of Independence and the adoption of the Second Amendment. See Brief for Professors of Linguistics and English as *Amici Curiae* 23–25. *Amici* determined that of 115 texts that employed the term, all but five usages were in a clearly military context, and in four of the remaining five instances, further qualifying language conveyed a different meaning.

ence to civilian uses of weapons tailors the text of the Amendment to the purpose identified in its preamble.[10]

The Court allows that the phrase "bear Arms" did have as an idiomatic meaning, " 'to serve as a soldier, do military service, fight,' " *ante,* at 12, but asserts that it *"unequivocally* bore that idiomatic meaning only when followed by the preposition 'against,' which was in turn followed by the target of the hostilities," *ante,* at 12–13. But contemporary sources make clear that the phrase "bear arms" was often used to convey a military meaning without those additional words. See, *e.g.,* To The Printer, Providence Gazette, (May 27, 1775) ("By the common estimate of three millions of people in America, allowing one in five to bear arms, there will be found 600,000 fighting men"); Letter of Henry Laurens to the Mass. Council (Jan. 21, 1778), in Letters of Delegates to Congress 1774–1789, p. 622 (P. Smith ed. 1981) ("Congress were yesterday informed . . . that those Canadians who returned from Saratoga . . . had been compelled by Sir Guy Carleton to bear Arms"); Of the Manner of Making War among the Indians of North-America, Connecticut Courant (May 23, 1785) ("The Indians begin to bear arms at the age of fifteen, and lay them aside when they arrive at the age of sixty. Some nations to the southward, I have been informed, do not continue their military exercises after they are fifty"); 28 Journals of the Continental Congress 1030 (G. Hunt ed. 1910) ("That hostages be mutually given as a security that the Convention troops and those received in exchange for them do not bear arms prior to the first day of May next"); H. R. J., 9th Cong., 1st Sess., 217 (Feb. 12, 1806) ("Whereas the commanders of British armed vessels have impressed many American seamen, and compelled them to bear arms on board said vessels, and assist in fighting their battles with nations in amity and peace with the United States"); H. R. J., 15th Cong., 2d Sess., 182–183 (Jan. 14, 1819) ("[The petitioners] state that they were residing in the British province of Canada, at the commencement of the late war, and that owing to their attachment to the United States, they refused to bear arms, when called upon by the British authorities . . .").

[10] *Aymette* v. *State,* 21 Tenn. 154, 156 (1840), a case we cited in *Miller,* further confirms this reading of the phrase. In *Aymette,* the Tennessee Supreme Court construed the guarantee in Tennessee's 1834 Constitution that " 'the free white men of this State, have a right to keep and bear arms for their common defence.' " Explaining that the provision was adopted with the same goals as the Federal Constitution's Second Amendment, the court wrote: "The words 'bear arms' . . . have reference to their military use, and were not employed to mean wearing them about the person as part of the dress. As the object for which the right

But when discussing these words, the Court simply ignores the preamble.

The Court argues that a "qualifying phrase that contradicts the word or phrase it modifies is unknown this side of the looking glass." *Ante,* at 15. But this fundamentally fails to grasp the point. The stand-alone phrase "bear arms" most naturally conveys a military meaning *unless* the addition of a qualifying phrase signals that a different meaning is intended. When, as in this case, there is no such qualifier, the most natural meaning is the military one; and, in the absence of any qualifier, it is all the more appropriate to look to the preamble to confirm the natural meaning of the text.[11] The Court's objection is particularly

----

to keep and bear arms is secured, is of general and public nature, to be exercised by the people in a body, for their *common defence,* so the *arms,* the right to keep which is secured, are such as are usually employed in civilized warfare, and that constitute the ordinary military equipment." 21 Tenn., at 158. The court elaborated: "[W]e may remark, that the phrase *'bear arms'* is used in the Kentucky Constitution as well as our own, and implies, as has already been suggested, their military use. . . . A man in the pursuit of deer, elk, and buffaloes, might carry his rifle every day, for forty years, and, yet, it would never be said of him, that he had *borne arms,* much less could it be said, that a private citizen *bears arms,* because he has a dirk or pistol concealed under his clothes, or a spear in a cane." *Id.,* at 161.

[11] As lucidly explained in the context of a statute mandating a sentencing enhancement for any person who "uses" a firearm during a crime of violence or drug trafficking crime:

"To use an instrumentality ordinarily means to use it for its intended purpose. When someone asks, 'Do you use a cane?,' he is not inquiring whether you have your grandfather's silver-handled walking stick on display in the hall; he wants to know whether you *walk* with a cane. Similarly, to speak of 'using a firearm' is to speak of using it for its distinctive purpose, *i.e.,* as a weapon. To be sure, one can use a firearm in a number of ways, including as an article of exchange, just as one can 'use' a cane as a hall decoration—but that is not the ordinary meaning of 'using' the one or the other. The Court does not appear to grasp the distinction between how a word *can be* used and how it *ordinarily* is used." *Smith* v. *United States,* 508 U. S. 223, 242 (1993) (SCALIA, J., dissenting) (some internal marks, footnotes, and citations

puzzling in light of its own contention that the addition of the modifier "against" changes the meaning of "bear arms." Compare *ante,* at 10 (defining "bear arms" to mean "carrying [a weapon] for a particular purpose— confrontation"), with *ante,* at 12 ("The phrase 'bear Arms' also had at the time of the founding an idiomatic meaning that was significantly different from its natural meaning: to serve as a soldier, do military service, fight or to wage war. But it unequivocally bore that idiomatic meaning only when followed by the preposition 'against.'" (citations and some internal quotation marks omitted)).

The Amendment's use of the term "keep" in no way contradicts the military meaning conveyed by the phrase "bear arms" and the Amendment's preamble. To the contrary, a number of state militia laws in effect at the time of the Second Amendment's drafting used the term "keep" to describe the requirement that militia members store their arms at their homes, ready to be used for service when necessary. The Virginia military law, for example, ordered that "every one of the said officers, non-commissioned officers, and privates, shall constantly *keep* the aforesaid arms, accoutrements, and ammunition, ready to be produced whenever called for by his commanding officer." Act for Regulating and Disciplining the Militia, 1785 Va. Acts ch. 1, §3, p. 2 (emphasis added).[12]

---

omitted).

[12] See also Act for the regulating, training, and arraying of the Militia, . . . of the State, 1781 N. J. Laws, ch. XIII, §12, p. 43 ("And be it Enacted, That each Person enrolled as aforesaid, shall also *keep* at his Place of Abode one Pound of good merchantable Gunpowder and three Pounds of Ball sized to his Musket or Rifle" (emphasis added)); An Act for establishing a Militia, 1785 Del. Laws §7, p. 59 ("*And be it enacted, That every person between the ages of eighteen and fifty* . . . shall at his own expense, provide himself . . . with a musket or firelock, with a bayonet, a cartouch box to contain twenty three cartridges, a priming wire, a brush and six flints, all in good order, on or before the first day of April next, under the penalty of forty shillings, and shall *keep* the

"[K]eep and bear arms" thus perfectly describes the responsibilities of a framing-era militia member.

This reading is confirmed by the fact that the clause protects only one right, rather than two. It does not describe a right "to keep arms" and a separate right "to bear arms." Rather, the single right that it does describe is both a duty and a right to have arms available and ready for military service, and to use them for military purposes when necessary.[13] Different language surely would have been used to protect nonmilitary use and possession of weapons from regulation if such an intent had played any role in the drafting of the Amendment.

*　　*　　*

When each word in the text is given full effect, the Amendment is most naturally read to secure to the people a right to use and possess arms in conjunction with service in a well-regulated militia. So far as appears, no more than that was contemplated by its drafters or is encompassed within its terms. Even if the meaning of the text were genuinely susceptible to more than one interpretation, the burden would remain on those advocating a departure from the purpose identified in the preamble and

---

same by him at all times, ready and fit for service, under the penalty of two shillings and six pence for each neglect or default thereof on every muster day" (second emphasis added)); 1782 Conn. Acts 590 ("And it shall be the duty of the Regional Quarter-Master to provide and *keep* a sufficient quantity of Ammunition and warlike stores for the use of their respective regiments, to be *kept* in such place or places as shall be ordered by the Field Officers" (emphasis added)).

[13] The Court notes that the First Amendment protects two separate rights with the phrase "the 'right [singular] of the people peaceably to assemble, and to petition the Government for a redress of grievances.'" *Ante*, at 18. But this only proves the point: In contrast to the language quoted by the Court, the Second Amendment does not protect a "right to keep *and to* bear arms," but rather a "right to keep and bear arms." The state constitutions cited by the Court are distinguishable on the same ground.

from settled law to come forward with persuasive new arguments or evidence. The textual analysis offered by respondent and embraced by the Court falls far short of sustaining that heavy burden.[14] And the Court's emphatic reliance on the claim "that the Second Amendment . . . codified a *pre-existing* right," *ante,* at 19, is of course beside the point because the right to keep and bear arms for service in a state militia was also a pre-existing right.

Indeed, not a word in the constitutional text even arguably supports the Court's overwrought and novel description of the Second Amendment as "elevat[ing] above all other interests" "the right of law-abiding, responsible citizens to use arms in defense of hearth and home." *Ante,* at 63.

II

The proper allocation of military power in the new Nation was an issue of central concern for the Framers. The compromises they ultimately reached, reflected in Article I's Militia Clauses and the Second Amendment, represent quintessential examples of the Framers' "splitting the atom of sovereignty."[15]

---

[14] The Court's atomistic, word-by-word approach to construing the Amendment calls to mind the parable of the six blind men and the elephant, famously set in verse by John Godfrey Saxe. The Poems of John Godfrey Saxe 135–136 (1873). In the parable, each blind man approaches a single elephant; touching a different part of the elephant's body in isolation, each concludes that he has learned its true nature. One touches the animal's leg, and concludes that the elephant is like a tree; another touches the trunk and decides that the elephant is like a snake; and so on. Each of them, of course, has fundamentally failed to grasp the nature of the creature.

[15] By "'split[ting] the atom of sovereignty,'" the Framers created "'two political capacities, one state and one federal, each protected from incursion by the other. The resulting Constitution created a legal system unprecedented in form and design, establishing two orders of government, each with its own direct relationship, its own privity, its own set of mutual rights and obligations to the people who sustain it

Two themes relevant to our current interpretive task ran through the debates on the original Constitution. "On the one hand, there was a widespread fear that a national standing Army posed an intolerable threat to individual liberty and to the sovereignty of the separate States." *Perpich* v. *Department of Defense,* 496 U. S. 334, 340 (1990).[16]   Governor Edmund Randolph, reporting on the Constitutional Convention to the Virginia Ratification Convention, explained: "With respect to a standing army, I believe there was not a member in the federal Convention, who did not feel indignation at such an institution." 3 J. Elliot, Debates in the Several State Conventions on the Adoption of the Federal Constitution 401 (2d ed. 1863) (hereinafter Elliot).   On the other hand, the Framers recognized the dangers inherent in relying on inadequately trained militia members "as the primary means of providing for the common defense," *Perpich,* 496 U. S., at 340; during the Revolutionary War, "[t]his force, though armed, was largely untrained, and its deficiencies were the subject of bitter complaint."   Wiener, The Militia Clause of the Constitution, 54 Harv. L. Rev. 181, 182 (1940).[17]   In order to respond to those twin concerns, a

———————

and are governed by it.'" *Saenz* v. *Roe,* 526 U. S. 489, 504, n. 17 (1999) (quoting *U. S. Term Limits, Inc.* v. *Thornton,* 514 U. S. 779, 838 (1995) (KENNEDY, J., concurring)).

[16] Indeed, this was one of the grievances voiced by the colonists: Paragraph 13 of the Declaration of Independence charged of King George, "He has kept among us, in times of peace, Standing Armies without the Consent of our legislatures."

[17] George Washington, writing to Congress on September 24, 1776, warned that for Congress "[t]o place any dependance upon Militia, is, assuredly, resting upon a broken staff." 6 Writings of George Washington 106, 110 (J. Fitzpatrick ed. 1932). Several years later he reiterated this view in another letter to Congress: "Regular Troops alone are equal to the exigencies of modern war, as well for defence as offence . . . . *No Militia* will ever acquire the habits necessary to resist a regular force. . . . The firmness requisite for the real business of fighting is only to be attained by a constant course of discipline and service." 20 *id.,* at

compromise was reached: Congress would be authorized to raise and support a national Army[18] and Navy, and also to organize, arm, discipline, and provide for the calling forth of "the Militia." U. S. Const., Art. I, §8, cls. 12–16. The President, at the same time, was empowered as the "Commander in Chief of the Army and Navy of the United States, and of the Militia of the several States, when called into the actual Service of the United States." Art. II, §2. But, with respect to the militia, a significant reservation was made to the States: Although Congress would have the power to call forth,[19] organize, arm, and discipline the militia, as well as to govern "such Part of them as may be employed in the Service of the United States," the States respectively would retain the right to appoint the officers and to train the militia in accordance with the discipline prescribed by Congress. Art. I, §8, cl. 16.[20]

49, 49–50 (Sept. 15, 1780). And Alexander Hamilton argued this view in many debates. In 1787, he wrote:

"Here I expect we shall be told that the militia of the country is its natural bulwark, and would be at all times equal to the national defense. This doctrine, in substance, had like to have lost us our independence. . . . War, like most other things, is a science to be acquired and perfected by diligence, by perseverance, by time, and by practice." The Federalist No. 25, p. 166 (C. Rossiter ed. 1961).

[18] "[B]ut no Appropriation of Money to that Use [raising and supporting Armies] shall be for a longer Term than two Years." U. S. Const., Art I, §8, cl. 12

[19] This "calling forth" power was only permitted in order for the militia "to execute the Laws of the Union, suppress Insurrections and repel Invasions." *Id.*, Art. I, §8, cl. 15.

[20] The Court assumes—incorrectly, in my view—that even when a state militia was not called into service, Congress would have had the power to exclude individuals from enlistment in that state militia. See *ante*, at 27. That assumption is not supported by the text of the Militia Clauses of the original Constitution, which confer upon Congress the power to "organiz[e], ar[m], and disciplin[e], the Militia," Art. I, §8, cl. 16, but not the power to say who will be members of a state militia. It is also flatly inconsistent with the Second Amendment. The States' power to create their own militias provides an easy answer to the

But the original Constitution's retention of the militia and its creation of divided authority over that body did not prove sufficient to allay fears about the dangers posed by a standing army. For it was perceived by some that Article I contained a significant gap: While it empowered Congress to organize, arm, and discipline the militia, it did not prevent Congress from providing for the militia's *disarmament*. As George Mason argued during the debates in Virginia on the ratification of the original Constitution:

> "The militia may be here destroyed by that method which has been practiced in other parts of the world before; that is, by rendering them useless—by disarming them. Under various pretences, Congress may neglect to provide for arming and disciplining the militia; and the state governments cannot do it, for Congress has the exclusive right to arm them." Elliot 379.

This sentiment was echoed at a number of state ratification conventions; indeed, it was one of the primary objections to the original Constitution voiced by its opponents. The Anti-Federalists were ultimately unsuccessful in persuading state ratification conventions to condition their approval of the Constitution upon the eventual inclusion of any particular amendment. But a number of States did propose to the first Federal Congress amendments reflecting a desire to ensure that the institution of the militia would remain protected under the new Government. The proposed amendments sent by the States of Virginia, North Carolina, and New York focused on the importance of preserving the state militias and reiterated the dangers posed by standing armies. New Hampshire sent a proposal that differed significantly from the others; while also

----

Court's complaint that the right as I have described it is empty because it merely guarantees "citizens' right to use a gun in an organization from which Congress has plenary authority to exclude them." *Ante,* at 28.

invoking the dangers of a standing army, it suggested that the Constitution should more broadly protect the use and possession of weapons, without tying such a guarantee expressly to the maintenance of the militia. The States of Maryland, Pennsylvania, and Massachusetts sent no relevant proposed amendments to Congress, but in each of those States a minority of the delegates advocated related amendments. While the Maryland minority proposals were exclusively concerned with standing armies and conscientious objectors, the unsuccessful proposals in both Massachusetts and Pennsylvania would have protected a more broadly worded right, less clearly tied to service in a state militia. Faced with all of these options, it is telling that James Madison chose to craft the Second Amendment as he did.

The relevant proposals sent by the Virginia Ratifying Convention read as follows:

> "17th, That the people have a right to keep and bear arms; that a well regulated Militia composed of the body of the people trained to arms is the proper, natural and safe defence of a free State. That standing armies are dangerous to liberty, and therefore ought to be avoided, as far as the circumstances and protection of the Community will admit; and that in all cases the military should be under strict subordination to and be governed by the civil power." Elliot 659.

> "19th. That any person religiously scrupulous of bearing arms ought to be exempted, upon payment of an equivalent to employ another to bear arms in his stead." *Ibid.*

North Carolina adopted Virginia's proposals and sent them to Congress as its own, although it did not actually ratify the original Constitution until Congress had sent the proposed Bill of Rights to the States for ratification. 2

Schwartz 932–933; see The Complete Bill of Rights 182–183 (N. Cogan ed. 1997) (hereinafter Cogan).

New York produced a proposal with nearly identical language. It read:

> "That the people have a right to keep and bear Arms; that a well regulated Militia, including the body of the People capable of bearing Arms, is the proper, natural, and safe defence of a free State. . . . That standing Armies, in time of Peace, are dangerous to Liberty, and ought not to be kept up, except in Cases of necessity; and that at all times, the Military should be kept under strict Subordination to the civil Power." 2 Schwartz 912.

Notably, each of these proposals used the phrase "keep and bear arms," which was eventually adopted by Madison. And each proposal embedded the phrase within a group of principles that are distinctly military in meaning.[21]

By contrast, New Hampshire's proposal, although it followed another proposed amendment that echoed the familiar concern about standing armies,[22] described the protection involved in more clearly personal terms. Its

---

[21] In addition to the cautionary references to standing armies and to the importance of civil authority over the military, each of the proposals contained a guarantee that closely resembled the language of what later became the Third Amendment. The 18th proposal from Virginia and North Carolina read "That no soldier in time of peace ought to be quartered in any house without the consent of the owner, and in time of war in such manner only as the law directs." Elliott 659. And New York's language read: "That in time of Peace no Soldier ought to be quartered in any House without the consent of the Owner, and in time of War only by the Civil Magistrate in such manner as the Laws may direct." 2 Schwartz 912.

[22] *"Tenth,* That no standing Army shall be Kept up in time of Peace unless with the consent of three fourths of the Members of each branch of Congress, nor shall Soldiers in Time of Peace be quartered upon private Houses with out the consent of the Owners."

proposal read:

> "*Twelfth,* Congress shall never disarm any Citizen unless such as are or have been in Actual Rebellion." *Id.,* at 758, 761.

The proposals considered in the other three States, although ultimately rejected by their respective ratification conventions, are also relevant to our historical inquiry. First, the Maryland proposal, endorsed by a minority of the delegates and later circulated in pamphlet form, read:

> "4. That no standing army shall be kept up in time of peace, unless with the consent of two thirds of the members present of each branch of Congress.

> .   .   .   .   .

> "10. That no person conscientiously scrupulous of bearing arms in any case, shall be compelled personally to serve as a soldier." *Id.,* at 729, 735.

The rejected Pennsylvania proposal, which was later incorporated into a critique of the Constitution titled "The Address and Reasons of Dissent of the Pennsylvania Minority of the Convention of the State of Pennsylvania to Their Constituents (1787)," signed by a minority of the State's delegates (those who had voted against ratification of the Constitution), *id.,* at 628, 662, read:

> 7. "That the people have a right to bear arms for the defense of themselves and their own State, or the United States, or for the purpose of killing game; and no law shall be passed for disarming the people or any of them unless for crimes committed, or real danger of public injury from individuals; and as standing armies in the time of peace are dangerous to liberty, they ought not to be kept up; and that the military shall be kept under strict subordination to, and be governed by the civil powers." *Id.,* at 665.

Finally, after the delegates at the Massachusetts Ratification Convention had compiled a list of proposed amendments and alterations, a motion was made to add to the list the following language: "[T]hat the said Constitution never be construed to authorize Congress to . . . prevent the people of the United States, who are peaceable citizens, from keeping their own arms." Cogan 181. This motion, however, failed to achieve the necessary support, and the proposal was excluded from the list of amendments the State sent to Congress. 2 Schwartz 674–675.

Madison, charged with the task of assembling the proposals for amendments sent by the ratifying States, was the principal draftsman of the Second Amendment.[23] He had before him, or at the very least would have been aware of, all of these proposed formulations. In addition, Madison had been a member, some years earlier, of the committee tasked with drafting the Virginia Declaration of Rights. That committee considered a proposal by Thomas Jefferson that would have included within the Virginia Declaration the following language: "No freeman shall ever be debarred the use of arms [within his own lands or tenements]." 1 Papers of Thomas Jefferson 363 (J. Boyd ed. 1950). But the committee rejected that language, adopting instead the provision drafted by George Mason.[24]

---

[23] Madison explained in a letter to Richard Peters, Aug. 19, 1789, the paramount importance of preparing a list of amendments to placate those States that had ratified the Constitution in reliance on a commitment that amendments would follow: "In many States the [Constitution] was adopted under a tacit compact in [favor] of some subsequent provisions on this head. In [Virginia]. It would have been *certainly* rejected, had no assurances been given by its advocates that such provisions would be pursued. As an honest man *I feel* my self bound by this consideration." Creating the Bill of Rights 281, 282 (H. Veit, K. Bowling, & C. Bickford eds. 1991) (hereinafter Veit).

[24] The adopted language, Virginia Declaration of Rights ¶13 (1776), read as follows: "That a well-regulated Militia, composed of the body of

With all of these sources upon which to draw, it is strikingly significant that Madison's first draft omitted any mention of nonmilitary use or possession of weapons. Rather, his original draft repeated the essence of the two proposed amendments sent by Virginia, combining the substance of the two provisions succinctly into one, which read: "The right of the people to keep and bear arms shall not be infringed; a well armed, and well regulated militia being the best security of a free country; but no person religiously scrupulous of bearing arms, shall be compelled to render military service in person." Cogan 169.

Madison's decision to model the Second Amendment on the distinctly military Virginia proposal is therefore revealing, since it is clear that he considered and rejected formulations that would have unambiguously protected civilian uses of firearms. When Madison prepared his first draft, and when that draft was debated and modified, it is reasonable to assume that all participants in the drafting process were fully aware of the other formulations that would have protected civilian use and possession of weapons and that their choice to craft the Amendment as they did represented a rejection of those alternative formulations.

Madison's initial inclusion of an exemption for conscientious objectors sheds revelatory light on the purpose of the Amendment. It confirms an intent to describe a duty as well as a right, and it unequivocally identifies the military character of both. The objections voiced to the conscientious-objector clause only confirm the central meaning of the text. Although records of the debate in the Senate, which is where the conscientious-objector clause was

---

the people, trained to arms, is the proper, natural, and safe defence of a free State; that Standing Armies, in time of peace, should be avoided as dangerous to liberty; and that, in all cases, the military should be under strict subordination to, and governed by, the civil power." 1 Schwartz 234.

removed, do not survive, the arguments raised in the House illuminate the perceived problems with the clause: Specifically, there was concern that Congress "can declare who are those religiously scrupulous, and prevent them from bearing arms."[25] The ultimate removal of the clause, therefore, only serves to confirm the purpose of the Amendment—to protect against congressional disarmament, by whatever means, of the States' militias.

The Court also contends that because "Quakers opposed the use of arms not just for militia service, but for any violent purpose whatsoever," *ante,* at 17, the inclusion of a conscientious-objector clause in the original draft of the Amendment does not support the conclusion that the phrase "bear arms" was military in meaning. But that claim cannot be squared with the record. In the proposals cited *supra,* at 21–22, both Virginia and North Carolina included the following language: "That any person religiously scrupulous of bearing arms ought to be exempted, upon payment of an equivalent *to employ another to bear arms in his stead*" (emphasis added).[26] There is no plausible argument that the use of "bear arms" in those provisions was not unequivocally and exclusively military: The State simply does not compel its citizens to carry arms for the purpose of private "confrontation," *ante,* at 10, or for self-defense.

The history of the adoption of the Amendment thus describes an overriding concern about the potential threat to state sovereignty that a federal standing army would

---

[25] Veit 182. This was the objection voiced by Elbridge Gerry, who went on to remark, in the next breath: "What, sir, is the use of a militia? It is to prevent the establishment of a standing army, the bane of liberty. . . . Whenever government mean to invade the rights and liberties of the people, they always attempt to destroy the militia, in order to raise an army upon their ruins." *Ibid.*

[26] The failed Maryland proposals contained similar language. See *supra,* at 23.

pose, and a desire to protect the States' militias as the means by which to guard against that danger. But state militias could not effectively check the prospect of a federal standing army so long as Congress retained the power to disarm them, and so a guarantee against such disarmament was needed.[27] As we explained in *Miller:* "With obvious purpose to assure the continuation and render possible the effectiveness of such forces the declaration and guarantee of the Second Amendment were made. It must be interpreted and applied with that end in view." 307 U. S., at 178. The evidence plainly refutes the claim that the Amendment was motivated by the Framers' fears that Congress might act to regulate any civilian uses of weapons. And even if the historical record were genuinely ambiguous, the burden would remain on the parties advocating a change in the law to introduce facts or arguments "'newly ascertained,'" *Vasquez,* 474 U. S., at 266; the Court is unable to identify any such facts or arguments.

III

Although it gives short shrift to the drafting history of the Second Amendment, the Court dwells at length on four other sources: the 17th-century English Bill of Rights; Blackstone's Commentaries on the Laws of England; postenactment commentary on the Second Amendment; and post-Civil War legislative history.[28] All of these

---

[27] The Court suggests that this historical analysis casts the Second Amendment as an "odd outlier," *ante,* at 30; if by "outlier," the Court means that the Second Amendment was enacted in a unique and novel context, and responded to the particular challenges presented by the Framers' federalism experiment, I have no quarrel with the Court's characterization.

[28] The Court's fixation on the last two types of sources is particularly puzzling, since both have the same characteristics as postenactment legislative history, which is generally viewed as the least reliable source of authority for ascertaining the intent of any provision's drafters. As has been explained:

sources shed only indirect light on the question before us, and in any event offer little support for the Court's conclusion.[29]

"The legislative history of a statute is the history of its consideration and enactment. 'Subsequent legislative history'—which presumably means the *post*-enactment history of a statute's consideration and enactment—is a contradiction in terms. The phrase is used to smuggle into judicial consideration legislators' expression *not* of what a bill currently under consideration means (which, the theory goes, reflects what their colleagues understood they were voting for), but of what a law *previously enacted* means. . . . In my opinion, the views of a legislator concerning a statute already enacted are entitled to no more weight than the views of a judge concerning a statute not yet passed." *Sullivan* v. *Finkelstein,* 496 U. S. 617, 631–632 (1990) (Scalia, J., concurring in part).

[29] The Court stretches to derive additional support from scattered state-court cases primarily concerned with state constitutional provisions. See *ante,* at 38–41. To the extent that those state courts assumed that the Second Amendment was coterminous with their differently worded state constitutional arms provisions, their discussions were of course dicta. Moreover, the cases on which the Court relies were decided between 30 and 60 years after the ratification of the Second Amendment, and there is no indication that any of them engaged in a careful textual or historical analysis of the federal constitutional provision. Finally, the interpretation of the Second Amendment advanced in those cases is not as clear as the Court apparently believes. In *Aldridge* v. *Commonwealth,* 2 Va. Cas. 447 (Gen. Ct. 1824), for example, a Virginia court pointed to the restriction on free blacks' "right to bear arms" as evidence that the protections of the State and Federal Constitutions did not extend to free blacks. The Court asserts that "[t]he claim was obviously not that blacks were prevented from carrying guns in the militia." *Ante,* at 39. But it is not obvious at all. For in many States, including Virginia, free blacks during the colonial period were prohibited from carrying guns in the militia, instead being required to "muste[r] without arms"; they were later barred from serving in the militia altogether. See Siegel, The Federal Government's Power to Enact Color-Conscious Laws: An Originalist Inquiry, 92 Nw. U. L. Rev. 477, 497–498, and n. 120 (1998). But my point is not that the *Aldridge* court endorsed my view of the Amendment—plainly it did not, as the premise of the relevant passage was that the Second Amendment applied to the States. Rather, my point is simply that the court could have understood the Second Amendment to protect a

The English Bill of Rights

The Court's reliance on Article VII of the 1689 English Bill of Rights—which, like most of the evidence offered by the Court today, was considered in *Miller*[30]—is misguided both because Article VII was enacted in response to different concerns from those that motivated the Framers of the Second Amendment, and because the guarantees of the two provisions were by no means coextensive. Moreover, the English text contained no preamble or other provision identifying a narrow, militia-related purpose.

The English Bill of Rights responded to abuses by the Stuart monarchs; among the grievances set forth in the Bill of Rights was that the King had violated the law "[b]y causing several good Subjects being Protestants to be disarmed at the same time when Papists were both armed and Employed contrary to Law." Article VII of the Bill of Rights was a response to that selective disarmament; it guaranteed that "the Subjects which are Protestants may have Armes for their defence, Suitable to their condition and as allowed by Law." L. Schwoerer, The Declaration of Rights, 1689 (App. 1, pp. 295, 297) (1981). This grant did

---

militia-focused right, and thus that its passing mention of the right to bear arms provides scant support for the Court's position.

[30] The Government argued in its brief that:

"[I]t would seem that the early English law did not guarantee an unrestricted right to bear arms. Such recognition as existed of a right in the people to keep and bear arms appears to have resulted from oppression by rulers who disarmed their political opponents and who organized large standing armies which were obnoxious and burdensome to the people. This right, however, it is clear, gave sanction only to the arming of the people as a body to defend their rights against tyrannical and unprincipled rulers. It did not permit the keeping of arms for purposes of private defense." Brief for United States in *United States* v. *Miller,* O. T. 1938, No. 696, pp. 11–12 (citations omitted). The Government then cited at length the Tennessee Supreme Court's opinion in *Aymette,* 21 Tenn. 154, which further situated the English Bill of Rights in its historical context. See n. 10, *supra.*

not establish a general right of all persons, or even of all Protestants, to possess weapons. Rather, the right was qualified in two distinct ways: First, it was restricted to those of adequate social and economic status ("suitable to their Condition"); second, it was only available subject to regulation by Parliament ("as allowed by Law").[31]

The Court may well be correct that the English Bill of Rights protected the right of *some* English subjects to use *some* arms for personal self-defense free from restrictions by the Crown (but not Parliament). But that right—adopted in a different historical and political context and framed in markedly different language—tells us little about the meaning of the Second Amendment.

Blackstone's Commentaries

The Court's reliance on Blackstone's Commentaries on the Laws of England is unpersuasive for the same reason as its reliance on the English Bill of Rights. Blackstone's invocation of "'the natural right of resistance and self-preservation,'" *ante,* at 20, and "'the right of having and using arms for self-preservation and defence'" *ibid.,* referred specifically to Article VII in the English Bill of Rights. The excerpt from Blackstone offered by the Court, therefore, is, like Article VII itself, of limited use in interpreting the very differently worded, and differently historically situated, Second Amendment.

What *is* important about Blackstone is the instruction he provided on reading the sort of text before us today. Blackstone described an interpretive approach that gave far more weight to preambles than the Court allows.

---

[31] Moreover, it was the Crown, not Parliament, that was bound by the English provision; indeed, according to some prominent historians, Article VII is best understood not as announcing any individual right to unregulated firearm ownership (after all, such a reading would fly in the face of the text), but as an assertion of the concept of parliamentary supremacy. See Brief for Jack N. Rakove et al. as *Amici Curiae* 6–9.

STEVENS, J., dissenting

Counseling that "[t]he fairest and most rational method to interpret the will of the legislator, is by exploring his intentions at the time when the law was made, by *signs* the most natural and probable," Blackstone explained that "[i]f words happen to be still dubious, we may establish their meaning from the context; with which it may be of singular use to compare a word, or a sentence, whenever they are ambiguous, equivocal, or intricate. Thus, the proeme, or preamble, is often called in to help the construction of an act of parliament." 1 Commentaries on the Laws of England 59–60 (1765) (hereinafter Blackstone). In light of the Court's invocation of Blackstone as "'the preeminent authority on English law for the founding generation,'" *ante,* at 20 (quoting *Alden* v. *Maine,* 527 U. S. 706, 715 (1999)), its disregard for his guidance on matters of interpretation is striking.

Postenactment Commentary

The Court also excerpts, without any real analysis, commentary by a number of additional scholars, some near in time to the framing and others post-dating it by close to a century. Those scholars are for the most part of limited relevance in construing the guarantee of the Second Amendment: Their views are not altogether clear,[32]

---

[32] For example, St. George Tucker, on whom the Court relies heavily, did not consistently adhere to the position that the Amendment was designed to protect the "Blackstonian" self-defense right, *ante,* at 33. In a series of unpublished lectures, Tucker suggested that the Amendment should be understood in the context of the compromise over military power represented by the original Constitution and the Second and Tenth Amendments:

"If a State chooses to incur the expense of putting arms into the Hands of its own Citizens for their defense, it would require no small ingenuity to prove that they have no right to do it, or that it could by any means contravene the Authority of the federal Govt. It may be alleged indeed that this might be done for the purpose of resisting the laws of the federal Government, or of shaking off the union: to which the plainest

they tended to collapse the Second Amendment with Article VII of the English Bill of Rights, and they appear to have been unfamiliar with the drafting history of the Second Amendment.[33]

The most significant of these commentators was Joseph Story. Contrary to the Court's assertions, however, Story actually supports the view that the Amendment was designed to protect the right of each of the States to maintain a well-regulated militia. When Story used the term "palladium" in discussions of the Second Amendment, he merely echoed the concerns that animated the Framers of the Amendment and led to its adoption. An excerpt from

------

answer seems to be, that whenever the States think proper to adopt either of these measures, they will not be with-held by the fear of infringing any of the powers of the federal Government. But to contend that such a power would be dangerous for the reasons above maintained would be subversive of every principle of Freedom in our Government; of which the first Congress appears to have been sensible by proposing an Amendment to the Constitution, which has since been ratified and has become part of it, viz., 'That a well regulated militia being necessary to the Security of a free State, the right of the people to keep and bear arms shall not be infringed.' To this we may add that this power of arming the militia, is not one of those prohibited to the States by the Constitution, and, consequently, is reserved to them under the twelfth Article of the ratified aments." S. Tucker, Ten Notebooks of Law Lectures, 1790's, Tucker-Coleman Papers, pp. 127–128 (College of William and Mary).

See also Cornell, St. George Tucker and the Second Amendment: Original Understandings and Modern Misunderstandings, 47 Wm. & Mary L. Rev. 1123 (2006).

[33] The Court does acknowledge that at least one early commentator described the Second Amendment as creating a right conditioned upon service in a state militia. See *ante,* at 37–38 (citing B. Oliver, The Rights of an American Citizen (1832)). Apart from the fact that Oliver is the *only* commentator in the Court's exhaustive survey who appears to have inquired into the intent of the drafters of the Amendment, what is striking about the Court's discussion is its failure to refute Oliver's description of the meaning of the Amendment or the intent of its drafters; rather, the Court adverts to simple nose-counting to dismiss his view.

his 1833 Commentaries on the Constitution of the United States—the same passage cited by the Court in *Miller*[34]—merits reproducing at some length:

> "The importance of [the Second Amendment] will scarcely be doubted by any persons who have duly reflected upon the subject. The militia is the natural defence of a free country against sudden foreign invasions, domestic insurrections, and domestic usurpations of power by rulers. It is against sound policy for a free people to keep up large military establishments and standing armies in time of peace, both from the enormous expenses with which they are attended and the facile means which they afford to ambitious and unprincipled rulers to subvert the government, or trample upon the rights of the people. The right of the citizens to keep and bear arms has justly been considered as the palladium of the liberties of a republic, since it offers a strong moral check against the usurpation and arbitrary power of rulers, and will generally, even if these are successful in the first instance, enable the people to resist and triumph over them. And yet, though this truth would seem so clear, and the importance of a well-regulated militia would seem so undeniable, it cannot be disguised that, among the American people, there is a growing indifference to any system of militia discipline, and a strong disposition, from a sense of its burdens, to be rid of all regulations. How it is practicable to keep the people duly armed without some organization, it is difficult to see. There is certainly no small danger that indifference may lead to disgust, and disgust to contempt; and thus gradually undermine all the protection intended by the clause of our national bill of rights." 2 J. Story, Commentaries on the Constitution of the United

---

[34]*Miller,* 307 U. S., at 182, n. 3.

States §1897, pp. 620–621 (4th ed. 1873) (footnote omitted).

Story thus began by tying the significance of the Amendment directly to the paramount importance of the militia. He then invoked the fear that drove the Framers of the Second Amendment—specifically, the threat to liberty posed by a standing army. An important check on that danger, he suggested, was a "well-regulated militia," *id.,* at 621, for which he assumed that arms would have to be kept and, when necessary, borne. There is not so much as a whisper in the passage above that Story believed that the right secured by the Amendment bore any relation to private use or possession of weapons for activities like hunting or personal self-defense.

After extolling the virtues of the militia as a bulwark against tyranny, Story went on to decry the "growing indifference to any system of militia discipline." *Ibid.* When he wrote, "[h]ow it is practicable to keep the people duly armed without some organization it is difficult to see," *ibid.,* he underscored the degree to which he viewed the arming of the people and the militia as indissolubly linked. Story warned that the "growing indifference" he perceived would "gradually undermine all the protection intended by this clause of our national bill of rights," *ibid.* In his view, the importance of the Amendment was directly related to the continuing vitality of an institution in the process of apparently becoming obsolete.

In an attempt to downplay the absence of any reference to nonmilitary uses of weapons in Story's commentary, the Court relies on the fact that Story characterized Article VII of the English Declaration of Rights as a "'similar provision,'" *ante,* at 36. The two provisions were indeed similar, in that both protected some uses of firearms. But Story's characterization in no way suggests that he believed that the provisions had the same scope. To the contrary, Story's exclusive focus on the militia in his discussion of the Second Amendment confirms his understanding of the right protected by the Second Amendment as limited to military uses of arms.

Story's writings as a Justice of this Court, to the extent that they shed light on this question, only confirm that Justice Story did not view the Amendment as conferring upon individuals any "self-defense" right disconnected from service in a state militia. Justice Story dissented from the Court's decision in *Houston* v. *Moore,* 5 Wheat. 1, 24 (1820), which held that a state court "had a concurrent jurisdiction" with the federal courts "to try a militia man who had disobeyed the call of the President, and to enforce the laws of Congress against such delinquent." *Id.,* at 31– 32. Justice Story believed that Congress' power to provide for the organizing, arming, and disciplining of the militia was, when Congress acted, plenary; but he explained that in the absence of congressional action, "I am certainly not prepared to deny the legitimacy of such an exercise of [state] authority." *Id.,* at 52. As to the Second Amendment, he wrote that it "may not, perhaps, be thought to have any important bearing on this point. If it have, it confirms and illustrates, rather than impugns the reasoning already suggested." *Id.,* at 52–53. The Court contends that had Justice Story understood the Amendment to have a militia purpose, the Amendment would have had "enormous and obvious bearing on the point." *Ante,* at 38. But the Court has it quite backwards: If Story had believed that the purpose of the Amendment was to permit civilians to keep firearms for activities like personal self-defense, what "confirm[ation] and illustrat[ion]," *Houston,* 5 Wheat., at 53, could the Amendment possibly have provided for the point that States retained the power to organize, arm, and discipline their own militias?

Post-Civil War Legislative History

The Court suggests that by the post-Civil War period, the Second Amendment was understood to secure a right to firearm use and ownership for purely private purposes like personal self-defense. While it is true that some of the legislative history on which the Court relies supports that contention, see *ante,* at 41–44, such sources are entitled to limited, if any, weight. All of the statements the Court cites were made long after the framing of the Amendment and cannot possibly supply any insight into the intent of the Framers; and all were made during pitched political debates, so that they are better characterized as advocacy than good-faith attempts at constitutional interpretation.

What is more, much of the evidence the Court offers is decidedly less clear than its discussion allows. The Court notes that "[b]lacks were routinely disarmed by Southern States after the Civil War. Those who opposed these injustices frequently stated that they infringed blacks' constitutional right to keep and bear arms." *Ante,* at 42. The Court hastily concludes that "[n]eedless to say, the claim was not that blacks were being prohibited from carrying arms in an organized state militia," *ibid.* But some of the claims of the sort the Court cites may have been just that. In some Southern States, Reconstruction-era Republican governments created state militias in which both blacks and whites were permitted to serve. Because "[t]he decision to allow blacks to serve alongside whites meant that most southerners refused to join the new militia," the bodies were dubbed "Negro militia[s]." S. Cornell, A Well-Regulated Militia 176–177 (2006). The "arming of the Negro militias met with especially fierce resistance in South Carolina. . . . The sight of organized, armed freedmen incensed opponents of Reconstruction and led to an intensified campaign of Klan terror. Leading members of the Negro militia were beaten or lynched and their weapons stolen." *Id.,* at 177.

One particularly chilling account of Reconstruction-era Klan violence directed at a black militia member is recounted in the memoir of Louis F. Post, A "Carpetbagger" in South Carolina, 10 Journal of Negro History 10 (1925). Post describes the murder by local Klan members of Jim Williams, the captain of a "Negro militia company," *id.*, at 59, this way:

> "[A] cavalcade of sixty cowardly white men, completely disguised with face masks and body gowns, rode up one night in March, 1871, to the house of Captain Williams . . . in the wood [they] hanged [and shot] him . . . [and on his body they] then pinned a slip of paper inscribed, as I remember it, with these grim words: 'Jim Williams gone to his last muster.'" *Id.*, at 61.

In light of this evidence, it is quite possible that at least some of the statements on which the Court relies actually did mean to refer to the disarmament of black militia members.

IV

The brilliance of the debates that resulted in the Second Amendment faded into oblivion during the ensuing years, for the concerns about Article I's Militia Clauses that generated such pitched debate during the ratification process and led to the adoption of the Second Amendment were short lived.

In 1792, the year after the Amendment was ratified, Congress passed a statute that purported to establish "an Uniform Militia throughout the United States." 1 Stat. 271. The statute commanded every able-bodied white male citizen between the ages of 18 and 45 to be enrolled therein and to "provide himself with a good musket or firelock" and other specified weaponry.[35] *Ibid.* The statute is significant, for it confirmed the way those in the founding generation viewed firearm ownership: as a duty linked to military service. The statute they enacted, however, "was virtually ignored for more than a century," and was finally repealed in 1901. See *Perpich,* 496 U. S., at 341.

The postratification history of the Second Amendment is strikingly similar. The Amendment played little role in any legislative debate about the civilian use of firearms for most of the 19th century, and it made few appearances in the decisions of this Court. Two 19th-century cases, however, bear mentioning.

In *United States* v. *Cruikshank,* 92 U. S. 542 (1876), the Court sustained a challenge to respondents' convictions under the Enforcement Act of 1870 for conspiring to deprive any individual of "'any right or privilege granted or secured to him by the constitution or laws of the United States.'" *Id.,* at 548. The Court wrote, as to counts 2 and 10 of respondents' indictment:

> "The right there specified is that of 'bearing arms for a lawful purpose.' This is not a right granted by the Constitution. Neither is it in any manner dependent on that instrument for its existence. The second amendment declares that it shall not be infringed; but this, as has been seen, means no more than that it shall not be infringed by Congress. This is one of the amendments that has no other effect than to restrict the powers of the national government." *Id.,* at 553.

---

[35] The additional specified weaponry included: "a sufficient bayonet and belt, two spare flints, and a knapsack, a pouch with a box therein to contain not less than twenty-four cartridges, suited to the bore of his musket or firelock, each cartridge to contain a proper quantity of powder and ball: or with a good rifle, knapsack, shot-pouch and powderhorn, twenty balls suited to the bore of his rifle and a quarter of a pound of powder." 1 Stat. 271.

The majority's assertion that the Court in *Cruikshank* "described the right protected by the Second Amendment as '"bearing arms for a lawful purpose,"'" *ante,* at 47 (quoting *Cruikshank,* 92 U. S., at 553), is not accurate. The *Cruikshank* Court explained that the defective *indictment* contained such language, but the Court did not itself describe the right, or endorse the indictment's description of the right.

Moreover, it is entirely possible that the basis for the indictment's counts 2 and 10, which charged respondents with depriving the victims of rights secured by the Second Amendment, was the prosecutor's belief that the victims— members of a group of citizens, mostly black but also white, who were rounded up by the Sheriff, sworn in as a posse to defend the local courthouse, and attacked by a white mob—bore sufficient resemblance to members of a state militia that they were brought within the reach of the Second Amendment. See generally C. Lane, The Day Freedom Died: The Colfax Massacre, The Supreme Court, and the Betrayal of Reconstruction (2008).

Only one other 19th-century case in this Court, *Presser* v. *Illinois,* 116 U. S. 252 (1886), engaged in any significant discussion of the Second Amendment. The petitioner in *Presser* was convicted of violating a state statute that prohibited organizations other than the Illinois National Guard from associating together as military companies or parading with arms. Presser challenged his conviction, asserting, as relevant, that the statute violated both the Second and the Fourteenth Amendments. With respect to the Second Amendment, the Court wrote:

> "We think it clear that the sections under consideration, which only forbid bodies of men to associate together as military organizations, or to drill or parade with arms in cities and towns unless authorized by law, do not infringe the right of the people to keep and

bear arms. But a conclusive answer to the contention that this amendment prohibits the legislation in question lies in the fact that the amendment is a limitation only upon the power of Congress and the National government, and not upon that of the States." *Id.,* at 264–265.

And in discussing the Fourteenth Amendment, the Court explained:

"The plaintiff in error was not a member of the organized volunteer militia of the State of Illinois, nor did he belong to the troops of the United States or to any organization under the militia law of the United States. On the contrary, the fact that he did not belong to the organized militia or the troops of the United States was an ingredient in the offence for which he was convicted and sentenced. The question is, therefore, had he a right as a citizen of the United States, in disobedience of the State law, to associate with others as a military company, and to drill and parade with arms in the towns and cities of the State? If the plaintiff in error has any such privilege he must be able to point to the provision of the Constitution or statutes of the United States by which it is conferred." *Id.,* at 266.

Presser, therefore, both affirmed *Cruikshank*'s holding that the Second Amendment posed no obstacle to regulation by state governments, and suggested that in any event nothing in the Constitution protected the use of arms outside the context of a militia "authorized by law" and organized by the State or Federal Government.[36]

---

[36] In another case the Court endorsed, albeit indirectly, the reading of *Miller* that has been well settled until today. In *Burton* v. *Sills,* 394 U. S. 812 (1969) *(per curiam),* the Court dismissed for want of a substantial federal question an appeal from a decision of the New Jersey

In 1901 the President revitalized the militia by creating "'the National Guard of the several States,'" *Perpich,* 496 U. S., at 341, and nn. 9–10; meanwhile, the dominant understanding of the Second Amendment's inapplicability to private gun ownership continued well into the 20th century. The first two federal laws directly restricting civilian use and possession of firearms—the 1927 Act prohibiting mail delivery of "pistols, revolvers, and other firearms capable of being concealed on the person," Ch. 75, 44 Stat. 1059, and the 1934 Act prohibiting the possession of sawed-off shotguns and machine guns—were enacted over minor Second Amendment objections dismissed by the vast majority of the legislators who participated in the debates.[37] Members of Congress clashed over the wisdom and efficacy of such laws as crime-control measures. But since the statutes did not infringe upon the military use or possession of weapons, for most legislators they did not even raise the specter of possible conflict with the Second Amendment.

Thus, for most of our history, the invalidity of Second-Amendment-based objections to firearms regulations has

---

Supreme Court upholding, against a Second Amendment challenge, New Jersey's gun control law. Although much of the analysis in the New Jersey court's opinion turned on the inapplicability of the Second Amendment as a constraint on the States, the court also quite correctly read *Miller* to hold that "Congress, though admittedly governed by the second amendment, may regulate interstate firearms so long as the regulation does not impair the maintenance of the active, organized militia of the states." *Burton* v. *Sills,* 53 N. J. 86, 98, 248 A. 2d 521, 527 (1968).

[37] The 1927 statute was enacted with no mention of the Second Amendment as a potential obstacle, although an earlier version of the bill had generated some limited objections on Second Amendment grounds; see 66 Cong. Rec. 725–735 (1924). And the 1934 Act featured just one colloquy, during the course of lengthy Committee debates, on whether the Second Amendment constrained Congress' ability to legislate in this sphere; see Hearings on House Committee on Ways and Means H. R. 9006, before the 73d Cong., 2d Sess., p. 19 (1934).

been well settled and uncontroversial.[38] Indeed, the Second Amendment was not even mentioned in either full House of Congress during the legislative proceedings that led to the passage of the 1934 Act. Yet enforcement of that law produced the judicial decision that confirmed the status of the Amendment as limited in reach to military usage. After reviewing many of the same sources that are discussed at greater length by the Court today, the *Miller* Court unanimously concluded that the Second Amendment did not apply to the possession of a firearm that did not have "some reasonable relationship to the preservation or efficiency of a well regulated militia." 307 U. S., at 178.

The key to that decision did not, as the Court belatedly suggests, *ante,* at 49–51, turn on the difference between

---

[38] The majority appears to suggest that even if the meaning of the Second Amendment has been considered settled by courts and legislatures for over two centuries, that settled meaning is overcome by the "reliance of millions of Americans" "upon the true meaning of the right to keep and bear arms." *Ante,* at 52, n. 24. Presumably by this the Court means that many Americans own guns for self-defense, recreation, and other lawful purposes, and object to government interference with their gun ownership. I do not dispute the correctness of this observation. But it is hard to see how Americans have "relied," in the usual sense of the word, on the existence of a constitutional right that, until 2001, had been rejected by every federal court to take up the question. Rather, gun owners have "relied" on the laws passed by democratically elected legislatures, which have generally adopted only limited gun-control measures.

Indeed, reliance interests surely cut the other way: Even apart from the reliance of judges and legislators who properly believed, until today, that the Second Amendment did not reach possession of firearms for purely private activities, "millions of Americans," have relied on the power of government to protect their safety and well-being, and that of their families. With respect to the case before us, the legislature of the District of Columbia has relied on its ability to act to "reduce the potentiality for gun-related crimes and gun-related deaths from occurring within the District of Columbia," H. Con. Res. 694, 94th Cong., 2d Sess., 25 (1976); see *post,* at 14–17 (BREYER, J., dissenting); so, too have the residents of the District.

muskets and sawed-off shotguns; it turned, rather, on the basic difference between the military and nonmilitary use and possession of guns. Indeed, if the Second Amendment were not limited in its coverage to military uses of weapons, why should the Court in *Miller* have suggested that some weapons but not others were eligible for Second Amendment protection? If use for self-defense were the relevant standard, why did the Court not inquire into the suitability of a particular weapon for self-defense purposes?

Perhaps in recognition of the weakness of its attempt to distinguish *Miller*, the Court argues in the alternative that *Miller* should be discounted because of its decisional history. It is true that the appellees in *Miller* did not file a brief or make an appearance, although the court below had held that the relevant provision of the National Firearms Act violated the Second Amendment (albeit without any reasoned opinion). But, as our decision in *Marbury* v. *Madison,* 1 Cranch 137, in which only one side appeared and presented arguments, demonstrates, the absence of adversarial presentation alone is not a basis for refusing to accord *stare decisis* effect to a decision of this Court. See Bloch, *Marbury* Redux, in Arguing *Marbury* v. *Madison* 59, 63 (M. Tushnet ed. 2005). Of course, if it can be demonstrated that new evidence or arguments were genuinely not available to an earlier Court, that fact should be given special weight as we consider whether to overrule a prior case. But the Court does not make that claim, because it cannot. Although it is true that the drafting history of the Amendment was not discussed in the Government's brief, see *ante,* at 51, it is certainly not the drafting history that the Court's decision today turns on. And those sources upon which the Court today relies most heavily *were* available to the *Miller* Court. The Government cited the English Bill of Rights and quoted a lengthy passage from *Aymette* detailing the history leading to the

English guarantee, Brief for United States in *United States* v. *Miller,* O. T. 1938, No. 696, pp 12–13; it also cited Blackstone, *id.,* at 9, n. 2, Cooley, *id.,* at 12, 15, and Story, *id.,* at 15. The Court is reduced to critiquing the number of *pages* the Government devoted to exploring the English legal sources. Only two (in a brief 21 pages in length)! Would the Court be satisfied with four? Ten?

The Court is simply wrong when it intones that *Miller* contained "*not a word*" about the Amendment's history. *Ante,* at 52. The Court plainly looked to history to construe the term "Militia," and, on the best reading of *Miller,* the entire guarantee of the Second Amendment. After noting the original Constitution's grant of power to Congress and to the States over the militia, the Court explained:

> "With obvious purpose to assure the continuation and render possible the effectiveness of such forces the declaration and guarantee of the Second Amendment were made. It must be interpreted and applied with that end in view.
>
> "The Militia which the States were expected to maintain and train is set in contrast with Troops which they were forbidden to keep without the consent of Congress. The sentiment of the time strongly disfavored standing armies; the common view was that adequate defense of country and laws could be secured through the Militia—civilians primarily, soldiers on occasion.
>
> "The signification attributed to the term Militia appears from the debates in the Convention, the history and legislation of Colonies and States, and the writings of approved commentators." *Miller,* 307 U. S., at 178–179.

The majority cannot seriously believe that the *Miller* Court did not consider any relevant evidence; the majority simply does not approve of the conclusion the *Miller* Court reached on that evidence. Standing alone, that is insufficient reason to disregard a unanimous opinion of this Court, upon which substantial reliance has been placed by legislators and citizens for nearly 70 years.

V

The Court concludes its opinion by declaring that it is not the proper role of this Court to change the meaning of rights "enshrine[d]" in the Constitution. *Ante,* at 64. But the right the Court announces was not "enshrined" in the Second Amendment by the Framers; it is the product of today's law-changing decision. The majority's exegesis has utterly failed to establish that as a matter of text or history, "the right of law-abiding, responsible citizens to use arms in defense of hearth and home" is "elevate[d] above all other interests" by the Second Amendment. *Ante,* at 64.

Until today, it has been understood that legislatures may regulate the civilian use and misuse of firearms so long as they do not interfere with the preservation of a well-regulated militia. The Court's announcement of a new constitutional right to own and use firearms for private purposes upsets that settled understanding, but leaves for future cases the formidable task of defining the scope of permissible regulations. Today judicial craftsmen have confidently asserted that a policy choice that denies a "law-abiding, responsible citize[n]" the right to keep and use weapons in the home for self-defense is "off the table." *Ante,* at 64. Given the presumption that most citizens are law abiding, and the reality that the need to defend oneself may suddenly arise in a host of locations outside the home, I fear that the District's policy choice may well be just the first of an unknown number of dominoes to be knocked off the table.[39]

I do not know whether today's decision will increase the labor of federal judges to the "breaking point" envisioned by Justice Cardozo, but it will surely give rise to a far more active judicial role in making vitally important national policy decisions than was envisioned at any time in the 18th, 19th, or 20th centuries.

The Court properly disclaims any interest in evaluating the wisdom of the specific policy choice challenged in this case, but it fails to pay heed to a far more important policy choice—the choice made by the Framers themselves. The Court would have us believe that over 200 years ago, the Framers made a choice to limit the tools available to elected officials wishing to regulate civilian uses of weapons, and to authorize this Court to use the common-law process of case-by-case judicial lawmaking to define the contours of acceptable gun control policy. Absent compelling evidence that is nowhere to be found in the Court's opinion, I could not possibly conclude that the Framers made such a choice.

For these reasons, I respectfully dissent.

---

[39] It was just a few years after the decision in *Miller* that Justice Frankfurter (by any measure a true judicial conservative) warned of the perils that would attend this Court's entry into the "political thicket" of legislative districting. *Colegrove* v. *Green,* 328 U. S. 549, 556 (1946) (plurality opinion). The equally controversial political thicket that the Court has decided to enter today is qualitatively different from the one that concerned Justice Frankfurter: While our entry into that thicket was justified because the political process was manifestly unable to solve the problem of unequal districts, no one has suggested that the political process is not working exactly as it should in mediating the debate between the advocates and opponents of gun control. What impact the Court's unjustified entry into *this* thicket will have on that ongoing debate—or indeed on the Court itself—is a matter that future historians will no doubt discuss at length. It is, however, clear to me that adherence to a policy of judicial restraint would be far wiser than the bold decision announced today.

SUPREME COURT OF THE UNITED STATES

No. 07–290

DISTRICT OF COLUMBIA, ET AL., PETITIONERS *v.*
DICK ANTHONY HELLER

ON WRIT OF CERTIORARI TO THE UNITED STATES COURT OF
APPEALS FOR THE DISTRICT OF COLUMBIA CIRCUIT

[June 26, 2008]

JUSTICE BREYER, with whom JUSTICE STEVENS, JUSTICE
SOUTER, and JUSTICE GINSBURG join, dissenting.

We must decide whether a District of Columbia law that
prohibits the possession of handguns in the home violates
the Second Amendment. The majority, relying upon its
view that the Second Amendment seeks to protect a right
of personal self-defense, holds that this law violates that
Amendment. In my view, it does not.

I

The majority's conclusion is wrong for two independent
reasons. The first reason is that set forth by JUSTICE
STEVENS—namely, that the Second Amendment protects
militia-related, not self-defense-related, interests. These
two interests are sometimes intertwined. To assure 18th-
century citizens that they could keep arms for militia
purposes would necessarily have allowed them to keep
arms that they could have used for self-defense as well.
But self-defense alone, detached from any militia-related
objective, is not the Amendment's concern.

The second independent reason is that the protection
the Amendment provides is not absolute. The Amendment
permits government to regulate the interests that it
serves. Thus, irrespective of what those interests are—
whether they do or do not include an independent interest

in self-defense—the majority's view cannot be correct unless it can show that the District's regulation is unreasonable or inappropriate in Second Amendment terms. This the majority cannot do.

In respect to the first independent reason, I agree with JUSTICE STEVENS, and I join his opinion. In this opinion I shall focus upon the second reason. I shall show that the District's law is consistent with the Second Amendment even if that Amendment is interpreted as protecting a wholly separate interest in individual self-defense. That is so because the District's regulation, which focuses upon the presence of handguns in high-crime urban areas, represents a permissible legislative response to a serious, indeed life-threatening, problem.

Thus I here assume that one objective (but, as the majority concedes, *ante*, at 26, not the *primary* objective) of those who wrote the Second Amendment was to help assure citizens that they would have arms available for purposes of self-defense. Even so, a legislature could reasonably conclude that the law will advance goals of great public importance, namely, saving lives, preventing injury, and reducing crime. The law is tailored to the urban crime problem in that it is local in scope and thus affects only a geographic area both limited in size and entirely urban; the law concerns handguns, which are specially linked to urban gun deaths and injuries, and which are the overwhelmingly favorite weapon of armed criminals; and at the same time, the law imposes a burden upon gun owners that seems proportionately no greater than restrictions in existence at the time the Second Amendment was adopted. In these circumstances, the District's law falls within the zone that the Second Amendment leaves open to regulation by legislatures.

II

The Second Amendment says that: "A well regulated

Militia, being necessary to the security of a free State, the right of the people to keep and bear Arms, shall not be infringed." In interpreting and applying this Amendment, I take as a starting point the following four propositions, based on our precedent and today's opinions, to which I believe the entire Court subscribes:

(1) The Amendment protects an "individual" right—*i.e.*, one that is separately possessed, and may be separately enforced, by each person on whom it is conferred. See, *e.g.*, *ante*, at 22 (opinion of the Court); *ante*, at 1 (STEVENS, J., dissenting).

(2) As evidenced by its preamble, the Amendment was adopted "[w]ith obvious purpose to assure the continuation and render possible the effectiveness of [militia] forces." *United States* v. *Miller*, 307 U. S. 174, 178 (1939); see *ante*, at 26 (opinion of the Court); *ante*, at 1 (STEVENS, J., dissenting).

(3) The Amendment "must be interpreted and applied with that end in view." *Miller, supra*, at 178.

(4) The right protected by the Second Amendment is not absolute, but instead is subject to government regulation. See *Robertson* v. *Baldwin*, 165 U. S. 275, 281–282 (1897); *ante*, at 22, 54 (opinion of the Court).

My approach to this case, while involving the first three points, primarily concerns the fourth. I shall, as I said, assume with the majority that the Amendment, in addition to furthering a militia-related purpose, also furthers an interest in possessing guns for purposes of self-defense, at least to some degree. And I shall then ask whether the Amendment nevertheless permits the District handgun restriction at issue here.

Although I adopt for present purposes the majority's position that the Second Amendment embodies a general concern about self-defense, I shall not assume that the Amendment contains a specific untouchable right to keep guns in the house to shoot burglars. The majority, which presents evidence in favor of the former proposition, does not, because it cannot, convincingly show that the Second Amendment seeks to maintain the latter in pristine, unregulated form.

To the contrary, colonial history itself offers important examples of the kinds of gun regulation that citizens would then have thought compatible with the "right to keep and bear arms," whether embodied in Federal or State Constitutions, or the background common law. And those examples include substantial regulation of firearms in urban areas, including regulations that imposed obstacles to the use of firearms for the protection of the home.

Boston, Philadelphia, and New York City, the three largest cities in America during that period, all restricted the firing of guns within city limits to at least some degree. See Churchill, Gun Regulation, the Police Power, and the Right to Keep Arms in Early America, 25 Law & Hist. Rev. 139, 162 (2007); Dept. of Commerce, Bureau of Census, C. Gibson, Population of the 100 Largest Cities and Other Urban Places in the United States: 1790 to 1990 (1998) (Table 2), online at http://www.census.gov/population/documentation/twps0027/tab02.txt (all Internet materials as visited June 19, 2008, and available in Clerk of Court's case file). Boston in 1746 had a law prohibiting the "discharge" of "any Gun or Pistol charged with Shot or Ball in the Town" on penalty of 40 shillings, a law that was later revived in 1778. See Act of May 28, 1746, ch. 10; An Act for Reviving and Continuing Sundry Laws that are Expired, and Near Expiring, 1778 Massachusetts Session Laws, ch. 5, pp. 193, 194. Philadelphia prohibited, on penalty of 5 shillings (or two days in jail if the fine were not paid), firing a gun or setting off fireworks in Philadelphia without a "governor's special license." See Act of Aug. 26, 1721, §4, in 3 Mitchell, Statutes at Large of Pennsylvania 253–254. And New York City banned, on penalty of a 20-shilling fine, the firing of guns (even in

Breyer, J., dissenting

houses) for the three days surrounding New Year's Day. 5 Colonial Laws of New York, ch. 1501, pp. 244–246 (1894); see also An Act to Suppress the Disorderly Practice of Firing Guns, & c., on the Times Therein Mentioned, 8 Statutes at Large of Pennsylvania 1770–1776, pp. 410–412 (1902) (similar law for all "inhabited parts" of Pennsylvania). See also An Act for preventing Mischief being done in the Town of *Newport*, or in any other Town in this Government, 1731, Rhode Island Session Laws (prohibiting, on penalty of 5 shillings for a first offense and more for subsequent offenses, the firing of "any Gun or Pistol . . . in the Streets of any of the Towns of this Government, or in any Tavern of the same, after dark, on any Night whatsoever").

Furthermore, several towns and cities (including Philadelphia, New York, and Boston) regulated, for fire-safety reasons, the storage of gunpowder, a necessary component of an operational firearm. See Cornell & DeDino, A Well Regulated Right, 73 Fordham L. Rev. 487, 510–512 (2004). Boston's law in particular impacted the use of firearms in the home very much as the District's law does today. Boston's gunpowder law imposed a £10 fine upon "any Person" who "shall take into any Dwelling-House, Stable, Barn, Out-house, Ware-house, Store, Shop, or other Building, within the Town of Boston, any . . . Fire-Arm, loaded with, or having Gun-Powder." An Act in Addition to the several Acts already made for the prudent Storage of Gun-Powder within the Town of Boston, ch. XIII, 1783 Mass. Acts 218–219; see also 1 S. Johnson, A Dictionary of the English Language 751 (4th ed. 1773) (defining "firearms" as "[a]rms which owe their efficacy to fire; guns"). Even assuming, as the majority does, see *ante*, at 59–60, that this law included an implicit self-defense exception, it would nevertheless have prevented a homeowner from keeping in his home a gun that he could immediately pick up and use against an intruder. Rather, the homeowner would have had to get the gunpowder and load it into the gun, an operation that would have taken a fair amount of time to perform. See Hicks, United States Military Shoulder Arms, 1795–1935, 1 Am. Military Hist. Foundation 23, 30 (1937) (experienced soldier could, with specially prepared cartridges as opposed to plain gunpowder and ball, load and fire musket 3-to-4 times per minute); *id.*, at 26–30 (describing the loading process); see also Grancsay, The Craft of the Early American Gunsmith, 6 Metropolitan Museum of Art Bulletin 54, 60 (1947) (noting that rifles were slower to load and fire than muskets).

Moreover, the law would, as a practical matter, have prohibited the carrying of loaded firearms anywhere in the city, unless the carrier had no plans to enter any building or was willing to unload or discard his weapons before going inside. And Massachusetts residents must have believed this kind of law compatible with the provision in the Massachusetts Constitution that granted "the people . . . a right to keep and to bear arms for the common defence"—a provision that the majority says was interpreted as "secur[ing] an individual right to bear arms for defensive purposes." Art. XVII (1780), in 3 The Federal and State Constitutions, Colonial Charters, and Other Organic Laws 1888, 1892 (F. Thorpe ed. 1909) (hereinafter Thorpe); *ante*, at 28–29 (opinion of the Court).

The New York City law, which required that gunpowder in the home be stored in certain sorts of containers, and laws in certain Pennsylvania towns, which required that gunpowder be stored on the highest story of the home, could well have presented similar obstacles to in-home use of firearms. See Act of April 13, 1784, ch. 28, 1784 N. Y. Laws p. 627; An Act for Erecting the Town of Carlisle, in the County of Cumberland, into a Borough, ch. XIV, §XLII, 1782 Pa. Laws p. 49; An Act for Erecting the Town of Reading, in the County of Berks, into a Borough, ch. LXXVI, §XLII, 1783 Pa. Laws p. 211. Although it is unclear whether these laws, like the Boston law, would have prohibited the storage of gunpowder inside a firearm, they would at the very least have made it difficult to reload the gun to fire a second shot unless the homeowner happened to be in the portion of the house where the extra gunpowder was required to be kept. See 7 United States Encyclopedia of History 1297 (P. Oehser ed. 1967) ("Until 1835 all small arms [were] single-shot weapons, requiring reloading by hand after every shot"). And Pennsylvania, like Massachusetts, had at the time one of the self-defense-guaranteeing state constitutional provisions on which the majority relies. See *ante*, at 28 (citing Pa. Declaration of Rights, Art. XIII (1776), in 5 Thorpe 3083).

The majority criticizes my citation of these colonial laws. See *ante*, at 59–62. But, as much as it tries, it cannot ignore their existence. I suppose it is possible that, as the majority suggests, see *ante*, at 59–61, they all in practice contained self-defense exceptions. But none of them expressly provided one, and the majority's assumption that such exceptions existed relies largely on the preambles to these acts—an interpretive methodology that it elsewhere roundly derides. Compare *ibid.* (interpreting 18th-century statutes in light of their preambles), with *ante*, at 4–5, and n. 3 (contending that the operative language of an 18th-century enactment may extend beyond its preamble). And in any event, as I have shown, the gunpowder-storage laws would have *burdened* armed self-defense, even if they did not completely *prohibit* it.

This historical evidence demonstrates that a self-defense assumption is the *beginning*, rather than the *end*, of any constitutional inquiry. That the District law impacts self-defense merely raises *questions* about the law's constitutionality. But to answer the questions that are raised (that is, to see whether the statute is unconstitutional) requires us to focus on practicalities, the statute's rationale, the problems that called it into being, its rela-

tion to those objectives—in a word, the details. There are
no purely logical or conceptual answers to such questions.
All of which to say that to raise a self-defense question is
not to answer it.

III

I therefore begin by asking a process-based question:
How is a court to determine whether a particular firearm
regulation (here, the District's restriction on handguns) is
consistent with the Second Amendment? What kind of
constitutional standard should the court use? How high a
protective hurdle does the Amendment erect?

The question matters. The majority is wrong when it
says that the District's law is unconstitutional "[u]nder
any of the standards of scrutiny that we have applied to
enumerated constitutional rights." *Ante,* at 56. How could
that be? It certainly would not be unconstitutional under,
for example, a "rational basis" standard, which requires a
court to uphold regulation so long as it bears a "rational
relationship" to a "legitimate governmental purpose."
Heller v. *Doe,* 509 U. S. 312, 320 (1993). The law at issue
here, which in part seeks to prevent gun-related accidents,
at least bears a "rational relationship" to that "legitimate"
life-saving objective. And nothing in the three 19th-
century state cases to which the majority turns for support
mandates the conclusion that the present District law
must fall. See *Andrews* v. *State,* 50 Tenn. 165, 177, 186–
187, 192 (1871) (striking down, as violating a *state* constitutional provision adopted in 1870, a *statewide* ban on a
carrying a broad class of weapons, insofar as it applied to
revolvers); *Nunn* v. *State,* 1 Ga. 243, 246, 250–251 (1846)
(striking down similarly broad ban on openly carrying
weapons, based on erroneous view that the Federal Second
Amendment applied to the States); *State* v. *Reid,* 1 Ala.
612, 614–615, 622 (1840) (*upholding* a concealed-weapon
ban against a *state* constitutional challenge). These cases

were decided well (80, 55, and 49 years, respectively) after the framing; they neither claim nor provide any special insight into the intent of the Framers; they involve laws much less narrowly tailored that the one before us; and state cases in any event are not determinative of federal constitutional questions, see, *e.g.*, *Garcia* v. *San Antonio Metropolitan Transit Authority*, 469 U. S. 528, 549 (1985) (citing *Martin* v. *Hunter's Lessee*, 1 Wheat. 304 (1816)).

Respondent proposes that the Court adopt a "strict scrutiny" test, which would require reviewing with care each gun law to determine whether it is "narrowly tailored to achieve a compelling governmental interest." *Abrams* v. *Johnson*, 521 U. S. 74, 82 (1997); see Brief for Respondent 54–62. But the majority implicitly, and appropriately, rejects that suggestion by broadly approving a set of laws—prohibitions on concealed weapons, forfeiture by criminals of the Second Amendment right, prohibitions on firearms in certain locales, and governmental regulation of commercial firearm sales—whose constitutionality under a strict scrutiny standard would be far from clear. See *ante*, at 54.

Indeed, adoption of a true strict-scrutiny standard for evaluating gun regulations would be impossible. That is because almost every gun-control regulation will seek to advance (as the one here does) a "primary concern of every government—a concern for the safety and indeed the lives of its citizens." *United States* v. *Salerno*, 481 U. S. 739, 755 (1987). The Court has deemed that interest, as well as "the Government's general interest in preventing crime," to be "compelling," see *id.*, at 750, 754, and the Court has in a wide variety of constitutional contexts found such public-safety concerns sufficiently forceful to justify restrictions on individual liberties, see *e.g.*, *Brandenburg* v. *Ohio*, 395 U. S. 444, 447 (1969) *(per curiam)* (First Amendment free speech rights); *Sherbert* v. *Verner*, 374 U. S. 398, 403 (1963) (First Amendment religious rights); *Brigham City* v. *Stuart*, 547 U. S. 398, 403–404 (2006) (Fourth Amendment protection of the home); *New York* v. *Quarles*, 467 U. S. 649, 655 (1984) (Fifth Amendment rights under *Miranda* v. *Arizona*, 384 U. S. 436 (1966)); *Salerno, supra*, at 755 (Eighth Amendment bail rights). Thus, any attempt *in theory* to apply strict scrutiny to gun regulations will *in practice* turn into an interest-balancing inquiry, with the interests protected by the Second Amendment on one side and the governmental public-safety concerns on the other, the only question being whether the regulation at issue impermissibly burdens the former in the course of advancing the latter.

I would simply adopt such an interest-balancing inquiry explicitly. The fact that important interests lie on both sides of the constitutional equation suggests that review of gun-control regulation is not a context in which a court should effectively presume either constitutionality (as in rational-basis review) or unconstitutionality (as in strict scrutiny). Rather, "where a law significantly implicates competing constitutionally protected interests in complex ways," the Court generally asks whether the statute burdens a protected interest in a way or to an extent that is out of proportion to the statute's salutary effects upon other important governmental interests. See *Nixon* v. *Shrink Missouri Government PAC*, 528 U. S. 377, 402 (2000) (BREYER, J., concurring). Any answer would take account both of the statute's effects upon the competing interests and the existence of any clearly superior less restrictive alternative. See *ibid.* Contrary to the majority's unsupported suggestion that this sort of "proportionality" approach is unprecedented, see *ante*, at 62, the Court has applied it in various constitutional contexts, including election-law cases, speech cases, and due process cases. See 528 U. S., at 403 (citing examples where the Court has taken such an approach); see also, *e.g., Thompson* v. *Western States Medical Center*, 535 U. S. 357, 388

(2002) (BREYER, J., dissenting) (commercial speech); *Burdick* v. *Takushi*, 504 U. S. 428, 433 (1992) (election regulation); *Mathews* v. *Eldridge*, 424 U. S. 319, 339–349 (1976) (procedural due process); *Pickering* v. *Board of Ed. of Township High School Dist. 205, Will Cty.*, 391 U. S. 563, 568 (1968) (government employee speech).

In applying this kind of standard the Court normally defers to a legislature's empirical judgment in matters where a legislature is likely to have greater expertise and greater institutional factfinding capacity. See *Turner Broadcasting System, Inc.* v. *FCC*, 520 U. S. 180, 195–196 (1997); see also *Nixon, supra,* at 403 (BREYER, J., concurring). Nonetheless, a court, not a legislature, must make the ultimate constitutional conclusion, exercising its "independent judicial judgment" in light of the whole record to determine whether a law exceeds constitutional boundaries. *Randall* v. *Sorrell*, 548 U. S. 230, 249 (2006) (opinion of BREYER, J.) (citing *Bose Corp.* v. *Consumers Union of United States, Inc.*, 466 U. S. 485, 499 (1984)).

The above-described approach seems preferable to a more rigid approach here for a further reason. Experience as much as logic has led the Court to decide that in one area of constitutional law or another the interests are likely to prove stronger on one side of a typical constitutional case than on the other. See, *e.g., United States* v. *Virginia*, 518 U. S. 515, 531–534 (1996) (applying heightened scrutiny to gender-based classifications, based upon experience with prior cases); *Williamson* v. *Lee Optical of Okla., Inc.*, 348 U. S. 483, 488 (1955) (applying rational-basis scrutiny to economic legislation, based upon experience with prior cases). Here, we have little prior experience. Courts that *do* have experience in these matters have uniformly taken an approach that treats empirically-based legislative judgment with a degree of deference. See Winkler, Scrutinizing the Second Amendment, 105 Mich. L. Rev. 683, 687, 716–718 (2007) (describing hundreds of gun-law decisions issued in the last half-century by Supreme Courts in 42 States, which courts with "surprisingly little variation," have adopted a standard more deferential than strict scrutiny). While these state cases obviously are not controlling, they are instructive. Cf., *e.g.*, *Bartkus* v. *Illinois*, 359 U. S. 121, 134 (1959) (looking to the "experience of state courts" as informative of a constitutional question). And they thus provide some comfort regarding the practical wisdom of following the approach that I believe our constitutional precedent would in any event suggest.

IV

The present suit involves challenges to three separate District firearm restrictions. The first requires a license from the District's Chief of Police in order to carry a "pistol," *i.e.*, a handgun, anywhere in the District. See D. C. Code §22–4504(a) (2001); see also §§22–4501(a), 22–4506. Because the District assures us that respondent could obtain such a license so long as he meets the statutory eligibility criteria, and because respondent concedes that those criteria are facially constitutional, I, like the majority, see no need to address the constitutionality of the licensing requirement. See *ante*, at 58–59.

The second District restriction requires that the lawful owner of a firearm keep his weapon "unloaded and disassembled or bound by a trigger lock or similar device" unless it is kept at his place of business or being used for lawful recreational purposes. See §7–2507.02. The only dispute regarding this provision appears to be whether the Constitution requires an exception that would allow someone to render a firearm operational when necessary for self-defense (*i.e.*, that the firearm may be operated under circumstances where the common law would normally permit a self-defense justification in defense against a criminal charge). See *Parker* v. *District of Columbia*, 478

F. 3d 370, 401 (2007) (case below); *ante*, at 57–58 (opinion of the Court); Brief for Respondent 52–54. The District concedes that such an exception exists. See Brief for Petitioners 56–57. This Court has final authority (albeit not often used) to definitively interpret District law, which is, after all, simply a species of federal law. See, *e.g.*, *Whalen* v. *United States*, 445 U. S. 684, 687–688 (1980); see also *Griffin* v. *United States*, 336 U. S. 704, 716–718 (1949). And because I see nothing in the District law that would *preclude* the existence of a background common-law self-defense exception, I would avoid the constitutional question by interpreting the statute to include it. See *Ashwander* v. *TVA*, 297 U. S. 288, 348 (1936) (Brandeis, J., concurring).

I am puzzled by the majority's unwillingness to adopt a similar approach. It readily reads unspoken self-defense exceptions into every colonial law, but it refuses to accept the District's concession that this law has one. Compare *ante*, at 59–61, with *ante*, at 57–58. The one District case it cites to support that refusal, *McIntosh* v. *Washington*, 395 A. 2d 744, 755–756 (1978), merely concludes that the District Legislature had a rational basis for applying the trigger-lock law in homes but not in places of business. Nowhere does that case say that the statute precludes a self-defense exception of the sort that I have just described. And even if it did, we are not bound by a lower court's interpretation of federal law.

The third District restriction prohibits (in most cases) the registration of a handgun within the District. See §7–2502.02(a)(4). Because registration is a prerequisite to firearm possession, see §7–2502.01(a), the effect of this provision is generally to prevent people in the District from possessing handguns. In determining whether this regulation violates the Second Amendment, I shall ask how the statute seeks to further the governmental interests that it serves, how the statute burdens the interests that the Second Amendment seeks to protect, and whether there are practical less burdensome ways of furthering those interests. The ultimate question is whether the statute imposes burdens that, when viewed in light of the statute's legitimate objectives, are disproportionate. See *Nixon*, 528 U. S., at 402 (Breyer, J., concurring).

A

No one doubts the constitutional importance of the statute's basic objective, saving lives. See, *e.g., Salerno*, 481 U. S., at 755. But there is considerable debate about whether the District's statute helps to achieve that objective. I begin by reviewing the statute's tendency to secure that objective from the perspective of (1) the legislature (namely, the Council of the District of Columbia) that enacted the statute in 1976, and (2) a court that seeks to evaluate the Council's decision today.

1

First, consider the facts as the legislature saw them when it adopted the District statute. As stated by the local council committee that recommended its adoption, the major substantive goal of the District's handgun restriction is "to reduce the potentiality for gun-related crimes and gun-related deaths from occurring within the District of Columbia." Hearing and Disposition before the House Committee on the District of Columbia, 94th Cong., 2d Sess., on H. Con. Res. 694, Ser. No. 94–24, p. 25 (1976) (herinafter DC Rep.) (reproducing, *inter alia,* the Council committee report). The committee concluded, on the basis of "extensive public hearings" and "lengthy research," that "[t]he easy availability of firearms in the United States has been a major factor contributing to the drastic increase in gun-related violence and crime over the past 40 years." *Id.,* at 24, 25. It reported to the Council "startling statistics," *id.,* at 26, regarding gun-related crime, accidents, and deaths, focusing particularly on the relation between handguns and crime and the proliferation of handguns within the District. See *id.,* at 25–26.

The committee informed the Council that guns were "responsible for 69 deaths in this country each day," for a total of "[a]pproximately 25,000 gun-deaths . . . each year," along with an additional 200,000 gun-related injuries. *Id.,* at 25. Three thousand of these deaths, the report stated, were accidental. *Ibid.* A quarter of the victims in those accidental deaths were children under the age of 14. *Ibid.* And according to the committee, "[f]or every intruder stopped by a homeowner with a firearm, there are 4 gun-related accidents within the home." *Ibid.*

In respect to local crime, the committee observed that there were 285 murders in the District during 1974—a record number. *Id.,* at 26. The committee also stated that, "[c]ontrary to popular opinion on the subject, fire-arms are more frequently involved in deaths and violence among relatives and friends than in premeditated criminal activities." *Ibid.* Citing an article from the American Journal of Psychiatry, the committee reported that "[m]ost murders are committed by previously law-abiding citizens, in situations where spontaneous violence is generated by anger, passion or intoxication, and where the killer and victim are acquainted." *Ibid.* "Twenty-five percent of these murders," the committee informed the Council, "occur within families." *Ibid.*

The committee report furthermore presented statistics strongly correlating handguns with crime. Of the 285 murders in the District in 1974, 155 were committed with handguns. *Ibid.* This did not appear to be an aberration, as the report revealed that "handguns [had been] used in roughly 54% of all murders" (and 87% of murders of law enforcement officers) nationwide over the preceding sev-eral years. *Ibid.* Nor were handguns only linked to mur-ders, as statistics showed that they were used in roughly

60% of robberies and 26% of assaults. *Ibid.* "A crime committed with a pistol," the committee reported, "is 7 times more likely to be lethal than a crime committed with any other weapon." *Id.*, at 25. The committee furthermore presented statistics regarding the availability of handguns in the United States, *ibid.*, and noted that they had "become easy for juveniles to obtain," even despite then-current District laws prohibiting juveniles from possessing them, *id.*, at 26.

In the committee's view, the current District firearms laws were unable "to reduce the potentiality for gun-related violence," or to "cope with the problems of gun control in the District" more generally. *Ibid.* In the absence of adequate federal gun legislation, the committee concluded, it "becomes necessary for local governments to act to protect their citizens, and certainly the District of Columbia as the only totally urban statelike jurisdiction should be strong in its approach." *Id.*, at 27. It recommended that the Council adopt a restriction on handgun registration to reflect "a legislative decision that, at this point in time and due to the gun-control tragedies and horrors enumerated previously" in the committee report, "pistols . . . are no longer justified in this jurisdiction." *Id.*, at 31; see also *ibid.* (handgun restriction "denotes a policy decision that handguns . . . have no legitimate use in the purely urban environment of the District").

The District's special focus on handguns thus reflects the fact that the committee report found them to have a particularly strong link to undesirable activities in the District's exclusively urban environment. See *id.*, at 25–26. The District did not seek to prohibit possession of other sorts of weapons deemed more suitable for an "urban area." See *id.*, at 25. Indeed, an original draft of the bill, and the original committee recommendations, had sought to prohibit registration of shotguns as well as handguns, but the Council as a whole decided to narrow the prohibition. Compare *id.,* at 30 (describing early version of the bill), with D. C. Code §7–2502.02).

2

Next, consider the facts as a court must consider them looking at the matter as of today. See, *e.g., Turner,* 520 U. S., at 195 (discussing role of court as factfinder in a constitutional case). Petitioners, and their *amici,* have presented us with more recent statistics that tell much the same story that the committee report told 30 years ago. At the least, they present nothing that would permit us to second-guess the Council in respect to the numbers of gun crimes, injuries, and deaths, or the role of handguns.

From 1993 to 1997, there were 180,533 firearm-related deaths in the United States, an average of over 36,000 per year. Dept. of Justice, Bureau of Justice Statistics, M. Zawitz & K. Strom, Firearm Injury and Death from Crime, 1993–97, p. 2 (Oct. 2000), online at http://www.ojp.usdoj.gov/bjs/pub/pdf/fidc9397.pdf (hereinafter Firearm Injury and Death from Crime). Fifty-one percent were suicides, 44% were homicides, 1% were legal interventions, 3% were unintentional accidents, and 1% were of undetermined causes. See *ibid.* Over that same period there were an additional 411,800 nonfatal firearm-related injuries treated in U. S. hospitals, an average of over 82,000 per year. *Ibid.* Of these, 62% resulted from assaults, 17% were unintentional, 6% were suicide attempts, 1% were legal interventions, and 13% were of unknown causes. *Ibid.*

The statistics are particularly striking in respect to children and adolescents. In over one in every eight firearm-related deaths in 1997, the victim was someone under the age of 20. American Academy of Pediatrics, Firearm-Related Injuries Affecting the Pediatric Population, 105 Pediatrics 888 (2000) (hereinafter Firearm-Related Injuries). Firearm-related deaths account for 22.5% of all injury deaths between the ages of 1 and 19. *Ibid.* More male teenagers die from firearms than from all natural causes combined. Dresang, Gun Deaths in Rural and Urban Settings, 14 J. Am. Bd. Family Practice 107 (2001). Persons under 25 accounted for 47% of hospital-treated firearm injuries between June 1, 1992 and May 31, 1993. Firearm-Related Injuries 891.

Handguns are involved in a majority of firearm deaths and injuries in the United States. *Id.,* at 888. From 1993 to 1997, 81% of firearm-homicide victims were killed by handgun. Firearm Injury and Death from Crime 4; see also Dept. of Justice, Bureau of Justice Statistics, C. Perkins, Weapon Use and Violent Crime, p. 8 (Sept. 2003), (Table 10), http://www.ojp.usdoj.gov/bjs/pub/pdf/wuvc01. pdf (hereinafter Weapon Use and Violent Crime) (statistics indicating roughly the same rate for 1993–2001). In the same period, for the 41% of firearm injuries for which the weapon type is known, 82% of them were from handguns. Firearm Injury and Death From Crime 4. And among children under the age of 20, handguns account for approximately 70% of all unintentional firearm-related injuries and deaths. Firearm-Related Injuries 890. In particular, 70% of all firearm-related teenage suicides in 1996 involved a handgun. *Id.,* at 889; see also Zwerling, Lynch, Burmeister, & Goertz, The Choice of Weapons in Firearm Suicides in Iowa, 83 Am. J. Public Health 1630, 1631 (1993) (Table 1) (handguns used in 36.6% of all firearm suicides in Iowa from 1980–1984 and 43.8% from 1990–1991).

Handguns also appear to be a very popular weapon among criminals. In a 1997 survey of inmates who were armed during the crime for which they were incarcerated, 83.2% of state inmates and 86.7% of federal inmates said that they were armed with a handgun. See Dept. of Justice, Bureau of Justice Statistics, C. Harlow, Firearm Use by Offenders, p. 3 (Nov. 2001), online at http://

www.ojp.usdoj.gov/bjs/pub/pdf/fuo.pdf; see also Weapon Use and Violent Crime 2 (Table 2) (statistics indicating that handguns were used in over 84% of nonlethal violent crimes involving firearms from 1993 to 2001). And handguns are not only popular tools for crime, but popular objects of it as well: the FBI received on average over 274,000 reports of stolen guns for each year between 1985 and 1994, and almost 60% of stolen guns are handguns. Dept. of Justice, Bureau of Justice Statistics, M. Zawitz, Guns Used in Crime, p. 3 (July 1995), online at http://www.ojp.usdoj.gov/bjs/pub/pdf/guic.pdf. Department of Justice studies have concluded that stolen handguns in particular are an important source of weapons for both adult and juvenile offenders. *Ibid.*

Statistics further suggest that urban areas, such as the District, have different experiences with gun-related death, injury, and crime, than do less densely populated rural areas. A disproportionate amount of violent and property crimes occur in urban areas, and urban criminals are more likely than other offenders to use a firearm during the commission of a violent crime. See Dept. of Justice, Bureau of Justice Statistics, D. Duhart, Urban, Suburban, and Rural Victimization, 1993–98, pp. 1, 9 (Oct. 2000), online at http://www.ojp.usdoj.gov/bjs/pub/pdf/ usrv98.pdf. Homicide appears to be a much greater issue in urban areas; from 1985 to 1993, for example, "half of all homicides occurred in 63 cities with 16% of the nation's population." Wintemute, The Future of Firearm Violence Prevention, 282 JAMA 475 (1999). One study concluded that although the overall rate of gun death between 1989 and 1999 was roughly the same in urban than rural areas, the urban homicide rate was three times as high; even after adjusting for other variables, it was still twice as high. Branas, Nance, Elliott, Richmond, & Schwab, Urban-Rural Shifts in Intentional Firearm Death, 94 Am. J. Public Health 1750, 1752 (2004); see also *ibid.* (noting that rural areas appear to have a higher rate of firearm suicide). And a study of firearm injuries to children and adolescents in Pennsylvania between 1987 and 2000 showed an injury rate in urban counties 10 times higher than in nonurban counties. Nance & Branas, The Rural-Urban Continuum, 156 Archives of Pediatrics & Adolescent Medicine 781, 782 (2002).

Finally, the linkage of handguns to firearms deaths and injuries appears to be much stronger in urban than in rural areas. "[S]tudies to date generally support the hypothesis that the greater number of rural gun deaths are from rifles or shotguns, whereas the greater number of urban gun deaths are from handguns." Dresang, *supra*, at 108. And the Pennsylvania study reached a similar conclusion with respect to firearm injuries—they are much more likely to be caused by handguns in urban areas than in rural areas. See Nance & Branas, *supra*, at 784.

3

Respondent and his many *amici* for the most part do not disagree about the *figures* set forth in the preceding subsection, but they do disagree strongly with the District's *predictive judgment* that a ban on handguns will help solve the crime and accident problems that those figures disclose. In particular, they disagree with the District Council's assessment that "freezing the pistol . . . population within the District," DC Rep., at 26, will reduce crime, accidents, and deaths related to guns. And they provide facts and figures designed to show that it has not done so in the past, and hence will not do so in the future.

First, they point out that, since the ban took effect, violent crime in the District has increased, not decreased. See Brief for Criminologists et al. as *Amici Curiae* 4–8, 3a (hereinafter Criminologists' Brief); Brief for Congress of Racial Equality as *Amicus Curiae* 35–36; Brief for National Rifle Assn. et al. as *Amici Curiae* 28–30 (hereinafter

NRA Brief). Indeed, a comparison with 49 other major cities reveals that the District's homicide rate is actually substantially *higher* relative to these other cities than it was before the handgun restriction went into effect. See Brief for Academics as *Amici Curiae* 7–10 (hereinafter Academics' Brief); see also Criminologists' Brief 6–9, 3a–4a, 7a. Respondent's *amici* report similar results in comparing the District's homicide rates during that period to that of the neighboring States of Maryland and Virginia (neither of which restricts handguns to the same degree), and to the homicide rate of the Nation as a whole. See Academics' Brief 11–17; Criminologists' Brief 6a, 8a.

Second, respondent's *amici* point to a statistical analysis that regresses murder rates against the presence or absence of strict gun laws in 20 European nations. See Criminologists' Brief 23 (citing Kates & Mauser, Would Banning Firearms Reduce Murder and Suicide? 30 Harv. J. L. & Pub. Pol'y 649, 651–694 (2007)). That analysis concludes that strict gun laws are correlated with *more* murders, not fewer. See Criminologists' Brief 23; see also *id.,* at 25–28. They also cite domestic studies, based on data from various cities, States, and the Nation as a whole, suggesting that a reduction in the number of guns does not lead to a reduction in the amount of violent crime. See *id.,* at 17–20. They further argue that handgun bans do not reduce suicide rates, see *id.,* at 28–31, 9a, or rates of accidents, even those involving children, see Brief for International Law Enforcement Educators and Trainers Assn. et al. as *Amici Curiae* App. 7–15 (hereinafter ILEETA Brief).

Third, they point to evidence indicating that firearm ownership does have a beneficial self-defense effect. Based on a 1993 survey, the authors of one study estimated that there were 2.2-to-2.5 million defensive uses of guns (mostly brandishing, about a quarter involving the actual firing of a gun) annually. See Kleck & Gertz,

Armed Resistance to Crime, 86 J. Crim. L. & C. 150, 164 (1995); see also ILEETA Brief App. 1–6 (summarizing studies regarding defensive uses of guns). Another study estimated that for a period of 12 months ending in 1994, there were 503,481 incidents in which a burglar found himself confronted by an armed homeowner, and that in 497,646 (98.8%) of them, the intruder was successfully scared away. See Ikida, Dahlberg, Sacks, Mercy, & Powell, Estimating Intruder-Related Firearms Retrievals in U. S. Households, 12 Violence & Victims 363 (1997). A third study suggests that gun-armed victims are substantially less likely than non-gun-armed victims to be injured in resisting robbery or assault. Barnett & Kates, Under Fire, 45 Emory L. J. 1139, 1243–1244, n. 478 (1996). And additional evidence suggests that criminals are likely to be deterred from burglary and other crimes if they know the victim is likely to have a gun. See Kleck, Crime Control Through the Private Use of Armed Force, 35 Social Problems 1, 15 (1988) (reporting a substantial drop in the burglary rate in an Atlanta suburb that required heads of households to own guns); see also ILEETA Brief 17–18 (describing decrease in sexual assaults in Orlando when women were trained in the use of guns).

Fourth, respondent's *amici* argue that laws criminalizing gun possession are self-defeating, as evidence suggests that they will have the effect only of restricting law-abiding citizens, but not criminals, from acquiring guns. See, *e.g.*, Brief for President *Pro Tempore* of Senate of Pennsylvania as *Amicus Curiae* 35, 36, and n. 15. That effect, they argue, will be especially pronounced in the District, whose proximity to Virginia and Maryland will provide criminals with a steady supply of guns. See Brief for Heartland Institute as *Amicus Curiae* 20.

In the view of respondent's *amici*, this evidence shows that other remedies—such as *less* restriction on gun ownership, or liberal authorization of law-abiding citizens to carry concealed weapons—better fit the problem. See, *e.g.*, Criminologists' Brief 35–37 (advocating easily obtainable gun licenses); Brief for Southeastern Legal Foundation, Inc. et al. as *Amici Curiae* 15 (hereinafter SLF Brief) (advocating "widespread gun ownership" as a deterrent to crime); see also J. Lott, More Guns, Less Crime (2d ed. 2000). They further suggest that at a minimum the District fails to show that its *remedy,* the gun ban, bears a reasonable relation to the crime and accident *problems* that the District seeks to solve. See, *e.g.*, Brief for Respondent 59–61.

These empirically based arguments may have proved strong enough to convince many legislatures, as a matter of legislative policy, not to adopt total handgun bans. But the question here is whether they are strong enough to destroy judicial confidence in the reasonableness of a legislature that rejects them. And that they are not. For one thing, they can lead us more deeply into the uncertainties that surround any effort to reduce crime, but they cannot prove either that handgun possession diminishes crime or that handgun bans are ineffective. The statistics do show a soaring District crime rate. And the District's crime rate went up after the District adopted its handgun ban. But, as students of elementary logic know, *after it* does not mean *because of it.* What would the District's crime rate have looked like without the ban? Higher? Lower? The same? Experts differ; and we, as judges, cannot say.

What about the fact that foreign nations with strict gun laws have higher crime rates? Which is the cause and which the effect? The proposition that strict gun laws *cause* crime is harder to accept than the proposition that strict gun laws in part grow out of the fact that a nation already has a higher crime rate. And we are then left with the same question as before: What would have happened to crime without the gun laws—a question that respondent and his *amici* do not convincingly answer.

Further, suppose that respondent's *amici* are right when they say that householders' possession of loaded handguns help to frighten away intruders. On that assumption, one must still ask whether that benefit is worth the potential death-related cost. And that is a question without a directly provable answer.

Finally, consider the claim of respondent's *amici* that handgun bans *cannot* work; there are simply too many illegal guns already in existence for a ban on legal guns to make a difference. In a word, they claim that, given the urban sea of pre-existing legal guns, criminals can readily find arms regardless. Nonetheless, a legislature might respond, we want to make an effort to try to dry up that urban sea, drop by drop. And none of the studies can show that effort is not worthwhile.

In a word, the studies to which respondent's *amici* point raise policy-related questions. They succeed in proving that the District's predictive judgments are controversial. But they do not by themselves show that those judgments are incorrect; nor do they demonstrate a consensus, academic or otherwise, supporting that conclusion.

Thus, it is not surprising that the District and its *amici* support the District's handgun restriction with studies of their own. One in particular suggests that, statistically speaking, the District's law has indeed had positive life-saving effects. See Loftin, McDowall, Weirsema, & Cottey, Effects of Restrictive Licensing of Handguns on Homicide and Suicide in the District of Columbia, 325 New England J. Med. 1615 (1991) (hereinafter Loftin study). Others suggest that firearm restrictions as a general matter reduce homicides, suicides, and accidents in the home. See, *e.g.*, Duggan, More Guns, More Crime, 109 J. Pol. Econ. 1086 (2001); Kellerman, Somes, Rivara, Lee, & Banton, Injuries and Deaths Due to Firearms in the Home, 45 J. Trauma, Infection & Critical Care 263 (1998);

Miller, Azrael, & Hemenway, Household Firearm Ownership and Suicide Rates in the United States, 13 Epidemiology 517 (2002). Still others suggest that the defensive uses of handguns are not as great in number as respondent's *amici* claim. See, *e.g.*, Brief for American Public Health Assn. et al. as *Amici Curiae* 17–19 (hereinafter APHA Brief) (citing studies).

Respondent and his *amici* reply to these responses; and in doing so, they seek to discredit as methodologically flawed the studies and evidence relied upon by the District. See, *e.g.*, Criminologists' Brief 9–17, 20–24; Brief for Assn. Am. Physicians and Surgeons, Inc. as *Amicus Curiae* 12–18; SLF Brief 17–22; Britt, Kleck, & Bordua, A Reassessment of the D.C. Gun Law, 30 Law & Soc. Rev. 361 (1996) (criticizing the Loftin study). And, of course, the District's *amici* produce counter-rejoinders, referring to articles that defend their studies. See, *e.g.*, APHA Brief 23, n. 5 (citing McDowall, Loftin, & Wiersema et al., Using Quasi-Experiments to Evaluate Firearm Laws, 30 Law & Soc. Rev. 381 (1996)).

The upshot is a set of studies and counterstudies that, at most, could leave a judge uncertain about the proper policy conclusion. But from respondent's perspective any such uncertainty is not good enough. That is because legislators, not judges, have primary responsibility for drawing policy conclusions from empirical fact. And, given that constitutional allocation of decisionmaking responsibility, the empirical evidence presented here is sufficient to allow a judge to reach a firm *legal* conclusion.

In particular this Court, in First Amendment cases applying intermediate scrutiny, has said that our "sole obligation" in reviewing a legislature's "predictive judgments" is "to assure that, in formulating its judgments," the legislature "has drawn reasonable inferences based on substantial evidence." *Turner*, 520 U. S., at 195 (internal quotation marks omitted). And judges, looking at the evidence before us, should agree that the District legislature's predictive judgments satisfy that legal standard. That is to say, the District's judgment, while open to question, is nevertheless supported by "substantial evidence."

There is no cause here to depart from the standard set forth in *Turner,* for the District's decision represents the kind of empirically based judgment that legislatures, not courts, are best suited to make. See *Nixon,* 528 U. S., at 402 (BREYER, J., concurring). In fact, deference to legislative judgment seems particularly appropriate here, where the judgment has been made by a local legislature, with particular knowledge of local problems and insight into appropriate local solutions. See *Los Angeles* v. *Alameda Books, Inc.,* 535 U. S. 425, 440 (2002) (plurality opinion) ("[W]e must acknowledge that the Los Angeles City Council is in a better position than the Judiciary to gather an evaluate data on local problems"); cf. DC Rep., at 67 (statement of Rep. Gude) (describing District's law as "a decision made on the local level after extensive debate and deliberations"). Different localities may seek to solve similar problems in different ways, and a "city must be allowed a reasonable opportunity to experiment with solutions to admittedly serious problems." *Renton* v. *Playtime Theatres, Inc.,* 475 U. S. 41, 52 (1986) (internal quotation marks omitted). "The Framers recognized that the most effective democracy occurs at local levels of government, where people with firsthand knowledge of local problems have more ready access to public officials responsible for dealing with them." *Garcia* v. *San Antonio Metropolitan Transit Authority,* 469 U. S. 528, 575, n. 18 (1985) (Powell, J., dissenting) (citing The Federalist No. 17, p. 107 (J. Cooke ed. 1961) (A. Hamilton)). We owe that democratic process some substantial weight in the constitutional calculus.

For these reasons, I conclude that the District's statute properly seeks to further the sort of life-preserving and public-safety interests that the Court has called "compelling." *Salerno*, 481 U. S., at 750, 754.

B

I next assess the extent to which the District's law burdens the interests that the Second Amendment seeks to protect. Respondent and his *amici*, as well as the majority, suggest that those interests include: (1) the preservation of a "well regulated Militia"; (2) safeguarding the use of firearms for sporting purposes, *e.g.*, hunting and marksmanship; and (3) assuring the use of firearms for self-defense. For argument's sake, I shall consider all three of those interests here.

1

The District's statute burdens the Amendment's first and primary objective hardly at all. As previously noted, there is general agreement among the Members of the Court that the principal (if not the only) purpose of the Second Amendment is found in the Amendment's text: the preservation of a "well regulated Militia." See *supra*, at 3. What scant Court precedent there is on the Second Amendment teaches that the Amendment was adopted "[w]ith obvious purpose to assure the continuation and render possible the effectiveness of [militia] forces" and "must be interpreted and applied with that end in view." *Miller*, 307 U. S., at 178. Where that end is implicated only minimally (or not at all), there is substantially less reason for constitutional concern. Compare *ibid.* ("In the absence of any evidence tending to show that possession or use of a 'shotgun having a barrel of less than eighteen inches in length' at this time has some reasonable relationship to the preservation or efficiency of a well regulated militia, we cannot say that the Second Amendment guarantees the right to keep and bear such an instrument").

To begin with, the present case has nothing to do with *actual* military service. The question presented presumes that respondent is "*not* affiliated with any state-regulated militia." 552 U. S. __ (2007) (emphasis added). I am aware of no indication that the District either now or in the recent past has called up its citizenry to serve in a militia, that it has any inkling of doing so anytime in the foreseeable future, or that this law must be construed to prevent the use of handguns during legitimate militia activities. Moreover, even if the District were to call up its militia, respondent would not be among the citizens whose service would be requested. The District does not consider him, at 66 years of age, to be a member of its militia. See D. C. Code §49–401 (2001) (militia includes only male residents ages 18 to 45); App. to Pet. for Cert. 120a (indicating respondent's date of birth).

Nonetheless, as some *amici* claim, the statute might interfere with training in the use of weapons, training useful for military purposes. The 19th-century constitutional scholar, Thomas Cooley, wrote that the Second Amendment protects "learning to handle and use [arms] in a way that makes those who keep them ready for their efficient use" during militia service. General Principles of Constitutional Law 271 (1880); *ante*, at 45 (opinion of the Court); see also *ante*, at 45–46 (citing other scholars agreeing with Cooley on that point). And former military officers tell us that "private ownership of firearms makes for a more effective fighting force" because "[m]ilitary recruits with previous firearms experience and training are generally better marksmen, and accordingly, better soldiers." Brief for Retired Military Officers as *Amici Curiae* 1–2 (hereinafter Military Officers' Brief). An *amicus* brief filed by retired Army generals adds that a "well-regulated militia—whether *ad hoc* or as part of our organized military—depends on recruits who have familiarity and training with firearms—rifles, pistols, and shotguns." Brief for

Major General John D. Altenburg, Jr., et al. as *Amici Curiae* 4 (hereinafter Generals' Brief). Both briefs point out the importance of handgun training. Military Officers' Brief 26–28; Generals' Brief 4. Handguns are used in military service, see *id.,* at 26, and "civilians who are familiar with handgun marksmanship and safety are much more likely to be able to safely and accurately fire a rifle or other firearm with minimal training upon entering military service," *id.,* at 28.

Regardless, to consider the military-training objective a modern counterpart to a similar militia-related colonial objective and to treat that objective as falling within the Amendment's primary purposes makes no difference here. That is because the District's law does not seriously affect military training interests. The law permits residents to engage in activities that will increase their familiarity with firearms. They may register (and thus possess in their homes) weapons other than handguns, such as rifles and shotguns. See D. C. Code §§7–2502.01, 7–2502.02(a) (only weapons that cannot be registered are sawed-off shotguns, machine guns, short-barreled rifles, and pistols not registered before 1976); compare Generals' Brief 4 (listing "*rifles*, pistols, and *shotguns*" as useful military weapons; emphasis added). And they may operate those weapons within the District "for lawful recreational purposes." §7–2507.02; see also §7–2502.01(b)(3) (nonresidents "participating in any lawful recreational firearm-related activity in the District, or on his way to or from such activity in another jurisdiction" may carry even weapons not registered in the District). These permissible recreations plainly include actually using and firing the weapons, as evidenced by a specific D. C. Code provision contemplating the existence of local firing ranges. See §7–2507.03.

And while the District law prevents citizens from training with handguns *within the District*, the District consists of only 61.4 square miles of urban area.   See Dept. of Commerce, Bureau of Census, United States: 2000 (pt. 1), p. 11 (2002) (Table 8).   The adjacent States do permit the use of handguns for target practice, and those States are only a brief subway ride away.   See Md. Crim. Law Code Ann. §4–203(b)(4) (Lexis Supp. 2007) (general handgun restriction does not apply to "the wearing, carrying, or transporting by a person of a handgun used in connection with," *inter alia,* "a target shoot, formal or informal target practice, sport shooting event, hunting, [or] a Department of Natural Resources-sponsored firearms and hunter safety class"); Va. Code Ann. §18.2–287.4 (Lexis Supp. 2007) (general restriction on carrying certain loaded pistols in certain public areas does not apply "to any person actually engaged in lawful hunting or lawful recreational shooting activities at an established shooting range or shooting contest"); Washington Metropolitan Area Transit Authority, Metrorail System Map, http://www.wmata.com/metrorail/systemmmap.cfm.

Of course, a subway rider must buy a ticket, and the ride takes time.   It also costs money to store a pistol, say, at a target range, outside the District.   But given the costs already associated with gun ownership and firearms training, I cannot say that a subway ticket and a short subway ride (and storage costs) create more than a minimal burden.   Compare *Crawford* v. *Marion County Election Bd.*, 553 U. S. ___, ___ (2008) (slip op., at 3) (BREYER, J., dissenting) (acknowledging travel burdens on indigent persons in the context of voting where public transportation options were limited).   Indeed, respondent and two of his coplaintiffs below may well use handguns outside the District on a regular basis, as their declarations indicate that they keep such weapons stored there.   See App. to Pet. for Cert. 77a (respondent); see also *id.,* at 78a, 84a (coplaintiffs).   I conclude that the District's law burdens the Second Amendment's primary objective little, or not at all.

2

The majority briefly suggests that the "right to keep and bear Arms" might encompass an interest in hunting. See, *e.g., ante,* at 26. But in enacting the present provisions, the District sought "to take nothing away from sportsmen." DC Rep., at 33. And any inability of District residents to hunt near where they live has much to do with the jurisdiction's exclusively urban character and little to do with the District's firearm laws. For reasons similar to those I discussed in the preceding subsection—that the District's law does not prohibit possession of rifles or shotguns, and the presence of opportunities for sporting activities in nearby States—I reach a similar conclusion, namely, that the District's law burdens any sports-related or hunting-related objectives that the Amendment may protect little, or not at all.

3

The District's law does prevent a resident from keeping a loaded handgun in his home. And it consequently makes it more difficult for the householder to use the handgun for self-defense in the home against intruders, such as burglars. As the Court of Appeals noted, statistics suggest that handguns are the most popular weapon for self defense. See 478 F. 3d, at 400 (citing Kleck & Gertz, 86 J. Crim. L. & C., at 182–183). And there are some legitimate reasons why that would be the case: *Amici* suggest (with some empirical support) that handguns are easier to hold and control (particularly for persons with physical infirmities), easier to carry, easier to maneuver in enclosed spaces, and that a person using one will still have a hand free to dial 911. See ILEETA Brief 37–39; NRA Brief 32–33; see also *ante,* at 57. But see Brief for Petitioners 54–55 (citing sources preferring shotguns and rifles to handguns for purposes of self-defense). To that extent the law burdens to some degree an interest in self-defense that for present purposes I have assumed the Amendment seeks to further.

C

In weighing needs and burdens, we must take account of the possibility that there are reasonable, but less restrictive alternatives. Are there *other* potential measures that might similarly promote the same goals while imposing lesser restrictions? See *Nixon*, 528 U. S., at 402 (BREYER, J., concurring) ("existence of a clearly superior, less restrictive alternative" can be a factor in determining whether a law is constitutionally proportionate). Here I see none.

The reason there is no clearly superior, less restrictive alternative to the District's handgun ban is that the ban's very objective is to reduce significantly the number of handguns in the District, say, for example, by allowing a law enforcement officer immediately to assume that *any* handgun he sees is an *illegal* handgun. And there is no plausible way to achieve that objective other than to ban the guns.

It does not help respondent's case to describe the District's objective more generally as an "effort to diminish the dangers associated with guns." That is because the very attributes that make handguns particularly useful for self-defense are also what make them particularly dangerous. That they are easy to hold and control means that they are easier for children to use. See Brief for American Academy of Pediatrics et al. as *Amici Curiae* 19 ("[C]hildren as young as three are able to pull the trigger of most handguns"). That they are maneuverable and permit a free hand likely contributes to the fact that they are by far the firearm of choice for crimes such as rape and robbery. See Weapon Use and Violent Crime 2 (Table 2).

That they are small and light makes them easy to steal, see *supra*, at 19, and concealable, cf. *ante*, at 54 (opinion of the Court) (suggesting that concealed-weapon bans are constitutional).

This symmetry suggests that any measure less restrictive in respect to the use of handguns for self-defense will, to that same extent, prove less effective in preventing the use of handguns for illicit purposes. If a resident has a handgun in the home that he can use for self-defense, then he has a handgun in the home that he can use to commit suicide or engage in acts of domestic violence. See *supra*, at 18 (handguns prevalent in suicides); Brief for National Network to End Domestic Violence et al. as *Amici Curiae* 27 (handguns prevalent in domestic violence). If it is indeed the case, as the District believes, that the number of guns contributes to the number of gun-related crimes, accidents, and deaths, then, although there may be less restrictive, *less effective* substitutes for an outright ban, there is no less restrictive *equivalent* of an outright ban.

Licensing restrictions would not similarly reduce the handgun population, and the District may reasonably fear that even if guns are initially restricted to law-abiding citizens, they might be stolen and thereby placed in the hands of criminals. See *supra*, at 19. Permitting certain types of handguns, but not others, would affect the commercial market for handguns, but not their availability. And requiring safety devices such as trigger locks, or imposing safe-storage requirements would interfere with any self-defense interest while simultaneously leaving operable weapons in the hands of owners (or others capable of acquiring the weapon and disabling the safety device) who might use them for domestic violence or other crimes.

The absence of equally effective alternatives to a complete prohibition finds support in the empirical fact that other States and urban centers prohibit particular types of weapons. Chicago has a law very similar to the District's, and many of its suburbs also ban handgun possession under most circumstances. See Chicago, Ill., Municipal Code §§8–20–030(k), 8–20–40, 8–20–50(c) (2008); Evanston, Ill., City Code §9–8–2 (2007); Morton Grove, Ill., Village Code §6–2–3(C) (2008); Oak Park, Ill., Village Code §27–2–1 (2007); Winnetka, Ill., Village Ordinance §9.12.020(B) (2008); Wilmette, Ill., Ordinance §12–24(b) (2008). Toledo bans certain types of handguns. Toledo, Ohio, Municipal Code, ch. 549.25 (2007). And San Francisco in 2005 enacted by popular referendum a ban on most handgun possession by city residents; it has been precluded from enforcing that prohibition, however, by state-court decisions deeming it pre-empted by state law. See *Fiscal* v. *City and County of San Francisco*, 158 Cal. App. 4th 895, 900–901, 70 Cal. Rptr. 3d 324, 326–328 (2008). (Indeed, the fact that as many as 41 States may pre-empt local gun regulation suggests that the absence of more regulation like the District's may perhaps have more to do with state law than with a lack of locally perceived need for them. See Legal Community Against Violence, Regulating Guns in America 14 (2006), http://www. lcav.org/Library/reports_analyses/National_Audit_Total_ 8.16.06.pdf.

In addition, at least six States and Puerto Rico impose general bans on certain types of weapons, in particular assault weapons or semiautomatic weapons. See Cal. Penal Code §12280(b) (West Supp. 2008); Conn. Gen. Stat. §§53–202c (2007); Haw. Rev. Stat. §134–8 (1993); Md. Crim. Law Code Ann. §4–303(a) (Lexis 2002); Mass. Gen. Laws, ch. 140, §131M (West 2006); N. Y. Penal Law Ann. §265.02(7) (West Supp. 2008); 25 Laws P. R. Ann. §456m (Supp. 2006); see also 18 U. S. C. §922(o) (federal machinegun ban). And at least 14 municipalities do the same. See Albany, N. Y., Municipal Code §193–16(A) (2005); Aurora, Ill., Ordinance §29–49(a) (2007); Buffalo,

N. Y., City Code §180–1(F) (2000); Chicago, Ill., Municipal Code §8–24–025(a), 8–20–030(h); Cincinnati, Ohio, Admin. Code §708–37(a) (Supp. 2008); Cleveland, Ohio, Ordinance §628.03(a) (2008); Columbus, Ohio, City Code §2323.31 (2007); Denver, Colo., Municipal Code §38–130(e) (2008); Morton Grove, Ill., Village Code §6–2–3(B); N. Y. C. Admin. Code §10–303.1 (2007); Oak Park, Ill., Village Code §27–2-1; Rochester, N. Y., Code §47–5(f) (2008); South Bend, Ind., Ordinance §§13–97(b), 13–98 (2008); Toledo, Ohio, Municipal Code §549.23(a). These bans, too, suggest that there may be no substitute to an outright prohibition in cases where a governmental body has deemed a particular type of weapon especially dangerous.

D

The upshot is that the District's objectives are compelling; its predictive judgments as to its law's tendency to achieve those objectives are adequately supported; the law does impose a burden upon any self-defense interest that the Amendment seeks to secure; and there is no clear less restrictive alternative. I turn now to the final portion of the "permissible regulation" question: Does the District's law *disproportionately* burden Amendment-protected interests? Several considerations, taken together, convince me that it does not.

First, the District law is tailored to the life-threatening problems it attempts to address. The law concerns one class of weapons, handguns, leaving residents free to possess shotguns and rifles, along with ammunition. The area that falls within its scope is totally urban. Cf. *Lorillard Tobacco Co.* v. *Reilly*, 533 U. S. 525, 563 (2001) (varied effect of statewide speech restriction in "rural, urban, or suburban" locales "demonstrates a lack of narrow tailoring"). That urban area suffers from a serious handgun-fatality problem. The District's law directly aims at that compelling problem. And there is no less restrictive way to achieve the problem-related benefits that it seeks.

Second, the self-defense interest in maintaining loaded handguns in the home to shoot intruders is not the *primary* interest, but at most a subsidiary interest, that the Second Amendment seeks to serve. The Second Amendment's language, while speaking of a "Militia," says nothing of "self-defense." As Justice Stevens points out, the Second Amendment's drafting history shows that the language reflects the Framers' primary, if not exclusive, objective. See *ante*, at 17–28 (dissenting opinion). And the majority itself says that "the threat that the new Federal Government would destroy the citizens' militia by taking away their arms was *the* reason that right . . . was codified in a written Constitution." *Ante*, at 26 (emphasis added). The *way* in which the Amendment's operative clause seeks to promote that interest—by protecting a right "to keep and bear Arms"—may *in fact* help further an interest in self-defense. But a factual connection falls far short of a primary objective. The Amendment itself tells us that militia preservation was first and foremost in the Framers' minds. See *Miller*, 307 U. S., at 178 ("With obvious purpose to assure the continuation and render possible the effectiveness of [militia] forces the declaration and guarantee of the Second Amendment were made," and the amendment "must be interpreted and applied with that end in view").

Further, any self-defense interest at the time of the Framing could not have focused exclusively upon urban-crime related dangers. Two hundred years ago, most Americans, many living on the frontier, would likely have thought of self-defense primarily in terms of outbreaks of fighting with Indian tribes, rebellions such as Shays' Rebellion, marauders, and crime-related dangers to travelers on the roads, on footpaths, or along waterways. See Dept. of Commerce, Bureau of Census, Population: 1790 to 1990 (1998) (Table 4), online at http://www.census.gov/

BREYER, J., dissenting

population/censusdata/table-4.pdf (of the 3,929,214 Americans in 1790, only 201,655—about 5%—lived in urban areas). Insofar as the Framers focused at all on the tiny fraction of the population living in large cities, they would have been aware that these city dwellers were subject to firearm restrictions that their rural counterparts were not. See *supra*, at 4–7. They are unlikely then to have thought of a right to keep loaded handguns in homes to confront intruders in urban settings as *central*. And the subsequent development of modern urban police departments, by diminishing the need to keep loaded guns nearby in case of intruders, would have moved any such right even further away from the heart of the amendment's more basic protective ends. See, *e.g.*, Sklansky, The Private Police, 46 UCLA L. Rev. 1165, 1206–1207 (1999) (professional urban police departments did not develop until roughly the mid-19th century).

Nor, for that matter, am I aware of any evidence that *handguns* in particular were central to the Framers' conception of the Second Amendment. The lists of militia-related weapons in the late 18th-century state statutes appear primarily to refer to other sorts of weapons, muskets in particular. See *Miller*, 307 U. S., at 180–182 (reproducing colonial militia laws). Respondent points out in his brief that the Federal Government and two States at the time of the founding had enacted statutes that listed handguns as "acceptable" militia weapons. Brief for Respondent 47. But these statutes apparently found them "acceptable" only for certain special militiamen (generally, certain soldiers on horseback), while requiring muskets or rifles for the general infantry. See Act of May 8, 1792, ch. XXXIII, 1 Stat. 271; Laws of the State of North Carolina 592 (1791); First Laws of the State of Connecticut 150 (1784); see also 25 Journals of the Continental Congress, pp. 1774–1789 741–742 (1922).

Third, irrespective of what the Framers *could have*

thought, we know what they *did think.* Samuel Adams, who lived in Boston, advocated a constitutional amendment that would have precluded the Constitution from ever being "construed" to "prevent the people of the United States, who are peaceable citizens, from keeping their own arms." 6 Documentary History of the Ratification of the Constitution 1453 (J. Kaminski & G. Saladino eds. 2000). Samuel Adams doubtless knew that the Massachusetts Constitution contained somewhat similar protection. And he doubtless knew that Massachusetts law prohibited Bostonians from keeping loaded guns in the house. So how could Samuel Adams have advocated such protection *unless* he thought that the protection was *consistent* with local regulation that seriously impeded urban residents from using their arms against intruders? It seems unlikely that he meant to deprive the Federal Government of power (to enact Boston-type weapons regulation) that he know Boston had and (as far as we know) he would have thought constitutional under the Massachusetts Constitution. Indeed, since the District of Columbia (the subject of the Seat of Government Clause, U. S. Const., Art. I, §8, cl. 17) was the only *urban* area under direct federal control, it seems unlikely that the Framers thought about *urban* gun control at all. Cf. *Palmore* v. *United States*, 411 U. S. 389, 397–398 (1973) (Congress can "legislate for the District in a manner with respect to subjects that would exceed its powers, or at least would be very unusual, in the context of national legislation enacted under other powers delegated to it").

Of course the District's law and the colonial Boston law are not identical. But the Boston law disabled an even wider class of weapons (indeed, all firearms). And its existence shows at the least that local legislatures could impose (as here) serious restrictions on the right to use firearms. Moreover, as I have said, Boston's law, though highly analogous to the District's, was not the *only* colonial law that could have impeded a homeowner's ability to shoot a burglar. Pennsylvania's and New York's laws could well have had a similar effect. See *supra*, at 6–7. And the Massachusetts and Pennsylvania laws were not only thought consistent with an *unwritten* common-law gun-possession right, but also consistent with *written* state constitutional provisions providing protections similar to those provided by the Federal Second Amendment. See *supra*, at 6–7. I cannot agree with the majority that these laws are largely uninformative because the penalty for violating them was civil, rather than criminal. *Ante*, at 61–62. The Court has long recognized that the exercise of a constitutional right can be burdened by penalties far short of jail time. See, *e.g.*, *Murdock* v. *Pennsylvania*, 319 U. S. 105 (1943) (invalidating $7 per week solicitation fee as applied to religious group); see also *Forsyth County* v. *Nationalist Movement*, 505 U. S. 123, 136 (1992) ("A tax based on the content of speech does not become more constitutional because it is a small tax").

Regardless, why would the majority require a precise colonial regulatory analogue in order to save a modern gun regulation from constitutional challenge? After all, insofar as we look to history to discover how we can constitutionally regulate a right to self-defense, we must look, not to what 18th-century legislatures actually *did* enact, but to what they would have thought they *could* enact. There are innumerable policy-related reasons why a legislature might not act on a particular matter, despite having the power to do so. This Court has "frequently cautioned that it is at best treacherous to find in congressional silence alone the adoption of a controlling rule of law." *United States* v. *Wells*, 519 U. S. 482, 496 (1997). It is similarly "treacherous" to reason from the fact that colonial legislatures *did not* enact certain kinds of legislation an unalterable constitutional limitation on the power of a modern legislature *cannot* do so. The question should not be whether a modern restriction on a right to self-defense *duplicates* a past one, but whether that restriction, when compared with restrictions originally thought possible, enjoys a similarly strong justification. At a minimum that similarly strong justification is what the District's modern law, compared with Boston's colonial law, reveals.

Fourth, a contrary view, as embodied in today's decision, will have unfortunate consequences. The decision will encourage legal challenges to gun regulation throughout the Nation. Because it says little about the standards used to evaluate regulatory decisions, it will leave the Nation without clear standards for resolving those challenges. See *ante*, at 54, and n. 26. And litigation over the course of many years, or the mere specter of such litigation, threatens to leave cities without effective protection against gun violence and accidents during that time.

As important, the majority's decision threatens severely to limit the ability of more knowledgeable, democratically elected officials to deal with gun-related problems. The majority says that it leaves the District "a variety of tools for combating" such problems. *Ante*, at 64. It fails to list even one seemingly adequate replacement for the law it strikes down. I can understand how reasonable individuals can disagree about the merits of strict gun control as a crime-control measure, even in a totally urbanized area. But I cannot understand how one can take from the elected branches of government the right to decide whether to insist upon a handgun-free urban populace in a city now facing a serious crime problem and which, in the future, could well face environmental or other emergencies that threaten the breakdown of law and order.

V

The majority derides my approach as "judge-empowering." *Ante*, at 62. I take this criticism seriously, but I do not think it accurate. As I have previously explained, this is an approach that the Court has taken in other areas of constitutional law. See *supra*, at 10–11. Application of such an approach, of course, requires judgment, but the very nature of the approach—requiring careful identification of the relevant interests and evaluating the law's effect upon them—limits the judge's choices; and the method's necessary transparency lays bare the judge's reasoning for all to see and to criticize.

The majority's methodology is, in my view, substantially less transparent than mine. At a minimum, I find it difficult to understand the reasoning that seems to underlie certain conclusions that it reaches.

The majority spends the first 54 pages of its opinion attempting to rebut JUSTICE STEVENS' evidence that the Amendment was enacted with a purely militia-related purpose. In the majority's view, the Amendment also protects an interest in armed personal self-defense, at least to some degree. But the majority does not tell us precisely what that interest is. "Putting all of [the Second Amendment's] textual elements together," the majority says, "we find that they guarantee the individual right to possess and carry weapons in case of confrontation." *Ante,* at 19. Then, three pages later, it says that "we do not read the Second Amendment to permit citizens to carry arms for *any sort* of confrontation." *Ante,* at 22. Yet, with one critical exception, it does not explain which confrontations count. It simply leaves that question unanswered.

The majority does, however, point to one type of confrontation that counts, for it describes the Amendment as "elevat[ing] above all other interests the right of law-abiding, responsible citizens to use arms in defense of hearth and home." *Ante,* at 63.   What is its basis for finding that to be the core of the Second Amendment right? The only historical sources identified by the majority that even appear to touch upon that specific matter consist of an 1866 newspaper editorial discussing the

Freedmen's Bureau Act, see *ante*, at 43, two quotations from that 1866 Act's legislative history, see *ante*, at 43–44, and a 1980 state court opinion saying that in colonial times the same were used to defend the home as to maintain the militia, see *ante*, at 52. How can citations such as these support the far-reaching proposition that the Second Amendment's primary concern is not its stated concern about the militia, but rather a right to keep loaded weapons at one's bedside to shoot intruders?

Nor is it at all clear to me how the majority decides *which* loaded "arms" a homeowner may keep. The majority says that that Amendment protects those weapons "typically possessed by law-abiding citizens for lawful purposes." *Ante*, at 53. This definition conveniently excludes machineguns, but permits handguns, which the majority describes as "the most popular weapon chosen by Americans for self-defense in the home." *Ante*, at 57; see also *ante,* at 54–55. But what sense does this approach make? According to the majority's reasoning, if Congress and the States lift restrictions on the possession and use of machineguns, and people buy machineguns to protect their homes, the Court will have to reverse course and find that the Second Amendment *does*, in fact, protect the individual self-defense-related right to possess a machinegun. On the majority's reasoning, if tomorrow someone invents a particularly useful, highly dangerous self-defense weapon, Congress and the States had better ban it immediately, for once it becomes popular Congress will no longer possess the constitutional authority to do so. In essence, the majority determines what regulations are permissible by looking to see what existing regulations permit. There is no basis for believing that the Framers intended such circular reasoning.

I am similarly puzzled by the majority's list, in Part III of its opinion, of provisions that in its view would survive Second Amendment scrutiny. These consist of (1) "prohibitions on carrying concealed weapons"; (2) "prohibitions on the possession of firearms by felons"; (3) "prohibitions on the possession of firearms by . . . the mentally ill"; (4) "laws forbidding the carrying of firearms in sensitive places such as schools and government buildings"; and (5) government "conditions and qualifications" attached "to the commercial sale of arms." *Ante*, at 54. Why these? Is it that similar restrictions existed in the late 18th century? The majority fails to cite any colonial analogues. And even were it possible to find analogous colonial laws in respect to all these restrictions, why should these colonial laws count, while the Boston loaded-gun restriction (along with the other laws I have identified) apparently does not count? See *supra*, at 5–6, 38–39.

At the same time the majority ignores a more important question: Given the purposes for which the Framers enacted the Second Amendment, how should it be applied to modern-day circumstances that they could not have anticipated? Assume, for argument's sake, that the Framers did intend the Amendment to offer a degree of self-defense protection. Does that mean that the Framers also intended to guarantee a right to possess a loaded gun near swimming pools, parks, and playgrounds? That they would not have cared about the children who might pick up a loaded gun on their parents' bedside table? That they (who certainly showed concern for the risk of fire, see *supra*, at 5–7) would have lacked concern for the risk of accidental deaths or suicides that readily accessible loaded handguns in urban areas might bring? Unless we believe that they intended future generations to ignore such matters, answering questions such as the questions in this case requires judgment—judicial judgment exercised within a framework for constitutional analysis that guides that judgment and which makes its exercise transparent. One cannot answer those questions by combining inconclusive historical research with judicial *ipse dixit*.

The argument about method, however, is by far the less important argument surrounding today's decision. Far more important are the unfortunate consequences that today's decision is likely to spawn. Not least of these, as I have said, is the fact that the decision threatens to throw into doubt the constitutionality of gun laws throughout the United States. I can find no sound legal basis for launching the courts on so formidable and potentially dangerous a mission. In my view, there simply is no untouchable constitutional right guaranteed by the Second Amendment to keep loaded handguns in the house in crime-ridden urban areas.

VI

For these reasons, I conclude that the District's measure is a proportionate, not a disproportionate, response to the compelling concerns that led the District to adopt it. And, for these reasons as well as the independently sufficient reasons set forth by JUSTICE STEVENS, I would find the District's measure consistent with the Second Amendment's demands.

With respect, I dissent.